THE
FORGOTTEN
EMPIRE

MOHENJO—DARO
AND THE ANCIENT INDUS LEGACY

WRITTEN BY ALISHAN PATEL
ILLUSTRATED BY SHEERAZ AHMED

Copyright 2025 by Alishan Patel

All rights reserved. No part of this publication may be reproduced, stored, or transmitted in any form or by any means, electronic, mechanical, photocopying, recording, scanning, or otherwise, without written permission from the author. It is illegal to copy this book, post it to a website, or distribute it by any other means without permission.

Alishan Patel asserts the moral right to be identified as the author of this work.

CONTENTS

Introduction: Rediscovering the Ancient Indus 1

Chapter One: The Birth of a Civilization 8

Chapter 2: Mohenjo-Daro Discovery and Excavation 16

Chapter 3: Urban Planning and Architecture 23

Chapter 4: Daily Life in Mohenjo-Daro 30

Chapter 5: Religion and Ritual 40

Chapter 6: Trade and Economy 50

Chapter 7: Art, Crafts, and Culture 61

Chapter 8: The Enigma of the Indus Script 72

Chapter Nine: Governance and Social Structure 83

Chapter Ten: Water, Sanitation, and Engineering 94

Chapter Eleven: Agriculture and Food Production 105

Chapter Twelve: Technology and Innovation 116

Chapter Thirteen: Relations with Contemporary Civilizations
.... 128

Chapter Fourteen: Theories of Decline and Abandonment 139

Chapter Fifteen: Modern Rediscovery and Archaeological Legacy 151

Chapter Sixteen: Preservation and Threats Today 162

Chapter Seventeen: Mohenjo-Daro in Popular Culture and Education 172

Chapter Eighteen: Future Research and Unanswered Questions 183

Conclusion: Legacy of the Indus Valley Civilization 194

INTRODUCTION: REDISCOVERING THE ANCIENT INDUS

A Civilization Lost to Time

Long before the famed philosophers of Athens posed questions about the cosmos, centuries before Rome's legions set foot across the known world, a sophisticated civilization flourished quietly along the alluvial plains of the Indus River. It left behind no epic poems, royal decrees, towering pyramids, or battle chronicles, yet what remains speaks volumes. The Indus Valley Civilization or Harappan Civilization, as it is also known, remains one of the most enigmatic and advanced early cultures in human history. Among its many urban marvels stood Mohenjo-Daro, a meticulously planned city that continues to astonish modern archaeologists and urban theorists alike.

When we speak of ancient history, we often look westward to the Nile, Mesopotamia, and the Mediterranean. The ruins of Mohenjo-Daro, however, whisper a different story: one of balance, order, innovation, and resilience. Unlike many other ancient cities that thrived on warfare or rigid hierarchies, Mohenjo-Daro reveals a society that prioritized cleanliness, commerce, civic organization, and, perhaps most intriguingly, anonymity over authoritarianism.

Unearthing Forgotten Splendor

The rediscovery of Mohenjo-Daro in the 1920s was nothing short of a revelation. British and Indian archaeologists, digging beneath the dusty plains of what is today modern-day Pakistan, began to piece together a civilization that predated even the earliest Vedic texts. What they found defied expectations: grid-patterned streets, sophisticated drainage systems, standardized brick dimensions, and multi-roomed homes that included private bathing areas around 2500 BCE.

This was not the work of a primitive or fragmented society. Mohenjo-Daro suggested a deeply organized civic life. It was an ancient city that understood the rhythm of human needs: privacy, hygiene, community, and commerce. Its rediscovery forced historians to redraw timelines and reconsider the cultural and technological capabilities of early South Asian civilizations.

The City as a Living Organism

To walk through the ruins of Mohenjo-Daro, even today, is to sense a profound intelligence in its layout. Streets were aligned with astonishing regularity. Houses were often built around central courtyards, and public structures hinted at communal gatherings and shared resources. The famed "Great Bath" suggests ritual purification or social harmony centered on cleanliness.

What is particularly striking is the absence of ostentatious temples or palaces. Unlike the ziggurats of Mesopotamia or the pyramids of Egypt, Mohenjo-Daro lacks the typical markers of divine kingship or central religious authority. This has led scholars to propose that its society might have been more egalitarian than its contemporaries. In a world where ancient cities often rose due to rigid class divisions and theocratic rule, Mohenjo-Daro flourished through civic cooperation and shared governance.

Trade, Technology, and Daily Life

Mohenjo-Daro was not an isolated marvel. It was part of a vast network of Harappan cities spread across the northwestern subcontinent. Its location on the lower Indus allowed it to be a trade hub, with evidence suggesting economic links stretching from Mesopotamia to Central Asia. Seals found at the site, inscribed with still-undeciphered script, were likely used in commercial transactions, hinting at a form of administration or regulatory oversight.

Craftsmanship, too, flourished. Artifacts recovered from Mohenjo-Daro include finely crafted pottery, toys, jewelry, and tools made from carnelian, bronze, and faience. These items, often found in domestic spaces, provide insight into everyday life, a life that blended utility with beauty, and personal comfort with community living.

Most fascinating, however, is the civilization's attention to water and sanitation. The extensive drainage and waste disposal systems of Mohenjo-Daro suggest a society acutely aware of public health and an understanding that would take other civilizations millennia to formalize.

A Silent Decline, a Lasting Legacy

And yet, for all its brilliance, Mohenjo-Daro did not last forever. By around 1900 BCE, the city and much of the Indus Valley

Civilization began to wane. The causes remain a subject of scholarly debate: climate change, shifting rivers, economic decline, or perhaps internal societal changes. No clear evidence of invasion or widespread destruction has been found. It is as if the city faded slowly, silently, absorbed back into the earth from which it rose.

Today, what remains is more than just broken bricks and buried streets. Mohenjo-Daro stands as a reminder that the roots of urban civilization are older and more diverse than many assume. Its rediscovery invites us to reassess how societies develop and what values they prioritize, whether conquest or cleanliness, spectacle or sustainability.

This book embarks on a journey through time, peeling back the layers of this extraordinary civilization. Through archaeology, scientific research, and historical interpretation, we will explore how Mohenjo-Daro was built, how its people lived, and what its rise

and decline can teach us about the arc of human civilization. It is not just a chronicle of the past; it is a mirror held up to the present, and perhaps, a subtle guide to the future.

CHAPTER ONE:
THE BIRTH OF A CIVILIZATION

Introduction

Long before the pyramids rose in Egypt or the ziggurats towered in Mesopotamia, an extraordinary culture began to emerge along the floodplains of the northwestern Indian subcontinent. This was the Indus Valley Civilization—one of the earliest cradles of human urban achievement. Known also as the Harappan Civilization, it flourished around 2600 BCE to 1900 BCE, encompassing a vast territory that stretched from present-day northeast Afghanistan to Pakistan and western India.

At its heart stood Mohenjo-Daro, a city of remarkable complexity and design. But before such cities could rise, a long process of environmental adaptation, agricultural innovation, and cultural development had to unfold. This chapter traces that journey—the prelude to urban greatness and civilization's birth.

1. The Land and the Rivers

The foundations of the Indus Valley Civilization were rooted in geography. The Indus River, flowing from the snowy peaks of the Himalayas and the Karakoram into the Arabian Sea, created one of the most fertile regions in the ancient world. Alongside it, the now-extinct Sarasvati (or Ghaggar-Hakra) River system provided crucial support to early settlements.

These rivers deposited rich alluvial soil, enabled seasonal irrigation, and sustained an environment ideal for farming. Unlike the unpredictable flooding of the Tigris or the Nile, the Indus offered relative stability. The predictable monsoon rains and fertile land allowed early communities to transition from nomadic lifestyles to settled agriculture.

The climate during the third millennium BCE was slightly wetter than today, supporting forests, wetlands, and wildlife that enriched human survival. In this ecologically diverse corridor, it was here that the earliest signs of complex society began to take root.

2. Early Settlements and Cultural Roots

The roots of the Indus Valley Civilization can be traced back to Neolithic farming villages such as Mehrgarh, located near the Bolan Pass in present-day Balochistan. As far back as 7000 BCE, Mehrgarh shows evidence of domesticated crops (like wheat and barley), cattle herding, and early ceramics.

From these humble beginnings, settlements gradually grew in size and complexity. By 4000 BCE, communities were engaging in:

- Pottery production
- Animal husbandry
- Trade of semi-precious stones and minerals
- Craft specialization, including bead-making and metallurgy

These formative stages are often referred to as the Pre-Harappan or Early Harappan period, and they laid the foundation for urbanism by introducing economic surplus, trade, and social organization.

3. The Rise of Cities

Around 2600 BCE, the Indus Valley witnessed a dramatic transformation. Dozens of urban centers emerged almost simultaneously across a vast territory, including Harappa, Mohenjo-Daro, Dholavira, Ganweriwala, and Lothal.

This phase—known as the Mature Harappan period—was marked by:

- Urban planning with streets laid out in grid patterns
- Standardized bricks and building techniques
- Complex drainage and water management systems
- Sophisticated craftsmanship and metallurgy
- Trade networks extending to Mesopotamia and Central Asia

These were not isolated cities. They shared a standard cultural template, evidenced by uniform seals, pottery styles, weights, and measures. Such consistency suggests a shared ideological framework or a highly interconnected economic and administrative system.

Unlike Egypt or Mesopotamia, the Indus cities lacked monumental religious or royal structures, suggesting a more egalitarian or decentralized governance model and a unique trajectory in early civilization.

4. Mohenjo-Daro: The Jewel of the Indus

Among all the cities in the Indus, Mohenjo-Daro stands out as a marvel of ancient engineering and social order. Located near the lower Indus River in present-day Sindh, Pakistan, the city covered an area of over 250 hectares and housed an estimated 30,000 to 50,000 people at its peak.

Its name, meaning "Mound of the Dead," is modern, and the original name remains lost. However, the archaeological evidence paints a vivid picture of:

- Wide, straight streets intersecting at right angles
- Public wells, baths, and granaries
- Residential quarters with private bathrooms and drainage
- A "citadel" area, possibly used for rituals or administration

Mohenjo-Daro encapsulated the culmination of centuries of innovation, demonstrating that the people of the Indus Valley had not only mastered their environment but had created one of the most organized and advanced urban societies of the ancient world.

Mound of the Dead, citadel

5. The Foundations of Civilization

The Indus Valley Civilization was more than a collection of cities. It was a complex cultural system underpinned by:

- Agriculture, using irrigation and crop rotation

- Artisan production, especially of ceramics, jewelry, and textiles

- Trade and exchange, supported by standardized weights and seals

- Cultural continuity, seen in motifs and urban forms across regions

Its people were literate, though their script remains undeciphered. They were technologically adept, socially organized, and environmentally adaptive. Most remarkably, they appear to have built their civilization without the hallmarks of coercion, such as standing armies or despotic rulers.

Conclusion: An Ancient Dawn

The birth of the Indus Valley Civilization is not merely the story of early cities; it is a testament to human ingenuity and cooperation. In the vast floodplains of South Asia, people learned to harness the rivers' rhythms, build communities rooted in order and resilience, and craft a legacy that continues to awe the modern world.

As we step forward into Mohenjo-Daro's story in the chapters ahead, we carry with us this sense of wonder at what humanity can achieve when it builds not for conquest, but for connection, sustainability, and shared life.

CHAPTER 2: MOHENJO-DARO DISCOVERY AND EXCAVATION

Introduction

Deep within the dusty plains of the Indus Valley, buried under layers of time and soil, lay the silent remnants of a lost civilization. For centuries, no one suspected that a sophisticated urban center had once flourished beneath these lands. The discovery of Mohenjo-Daro, one of the principal settlements of the Indus Valley Civilization, forever altered our understanding of ancient human history. This chapter takes you through the fascinating story of its discovery, the methodical efforts of excavation, and the profound impact it had on archaeology and the study of early civilizations.

1. The Road to Discovery

The journey toward uncovering Mohenjo-Daro began in the early 20th century, when British colonial interests in India were intensifying archaeological investigations. Although scattered reports of unusual brick structures had circulated in the 19th century, it was not until 1922 that the site truly captured the attention of the archaeological community.

Rakhaldas Banerji, an officer of the Archaeological Survey of India (ASI), was stationed at the site of ancient Buddhist ruins in Sindh (modern-day Pakistan) when he noticed some peculiar mounds and unusually baked bricks that seemed to predate the Buddhist remains. His curiosity led to preliminary digs and eventually to the realization that this was no ordinary ancient site.

What Banerji and his colleagues unearthed would soon lead to one of the most important archaeological discoveries of the 20th century. The mounds, known locally as Mohenjo-Daro, or "Mound of the Dead," held secrets of an ancient urban culture long forgotten by time.

2. The First Excavations

The initial excavations began in earnest under the supervision of Sir John Marshall, then Director-General of the Archaeological Survey of India. Between 1922 and 1927, large-scale digs revealed a remarkably well-planned city. The excavation team, including notable figures like K.N. Dikshit, E.J.H. MacKay, and Madho Sarup Vats, worked through difficult conditions to peel back the soil layers and uncover a thriving city that had once housed tens of thousands of people.

The city's layout astonished archaeologists: a highly organized grid system, baked brick houses, drainage systems, public baths, and granaries emerged from the earth. The advanced town planning suggested a level of civic administration and urban sophistication unparalleled in any civilization of that period.

Each trench, wall, and artifact told a part of the story. Tools, pottery, seals, figurines, and even food remnants offered glimpses into a culture that valued cleanliness, trade, and community living. It was clear that Mohenjo-Daro was more than just an ancient settlement; it was a jewel of antiquity.

3. Unraveling the City's Structure

As excavations progressed, Mohenjo-Daro revealed itself as a city of two distinct sections: the Citadel and the Lower City.

The Citadel, built on a raised platform, is believed to have been the seat of administrative and perhaps religious authority. The famous Great Bath stood within it, a large, watertight structure that may have served ritual or communal purposes. Surrounding buildings, such as granaries and assembly halls, suggest a high level of political organization and resource management.

The Lower City was composed of residential buildings, markets, and workshops. The layout reflected an early understanding of city zoning. Streets intersected at right angles, and most homes were equipped with private wells, bathrooms, and covered drainage, a remarkable achievement in sanitation.

This systematic urban planning and the absence of palaces or temples posed intriguing questions. Who ruled this city? Was it governed by a collective or a priestly class? The answers remained elusive, buried alongside the ruins.

4. Challenges in Excavation

Excavating Mohenjo-Daro presented significant challenges. Seasonal flooding from the Indus River constantly threatened the site, and the high-water table limited the depth to which archaeologists could dig. Moreover, early excavation techniques lacked modern archaeology's precision and preservation standards, leading to damage and loss of context for many artifacts.

Another difficulty was the sheer scale of the city. With over 200 hectares of ruins, only a small portion of Mohenjo-Daro has been excavated, and much of the site remains untouched, protected under government preservation efforts to prevent further degradation.

Despite these obstacles, the work done in the early 20th century laid a solid foundation for future archaeological studies and ignited global interest in the Indus Valley Civilization.

5. Legacy and Significance

The discovery and excavation of Mohenjo-Daro redefined the timeline and scope of ancient urban civilizations. Before this, it was widely believed that the earliest cities arose in Mesopotamia and Egypt. Mohenjo-Daro, dating back to around 2600 BCE, proved that complex urban centers had also developed independently in South Asia.

More importantly, it revealed a civilization characterized by peace, planning, and prosperity. The absence of large-scale weapons, military structures, or evidence of widespread warfare suggested a society that may have been remarkably stable and cooperative.

In recognition of its immense value, Mohenjo-Daro was designated a UNESCO World Heritage Site in 1980. It inspires historians, archaeologists, and the general public, offering timeless lessons in sustainability, governance, and human ingenuity.

Conclusion

Mohenjo-Daro remains one of archaeology's most fascinating stories, a buried city whose rediscovery challenged long-held assumptions and illuminated a lost chapter of human history. From its chance discovery to its painstaking excavation, every layer of earth removed brought humanity closer to understanding one of its oldest and most enigmatic urban societies.

Though many questions remain unanswered about its language, people, and ultimate decline, Mohenjo-Daro stands as a testament to the enduring legacy of the Indus Valley Civilization. The city, once lost beneath the dust of time, now lives on in the chronicles of world heritage and the minds of all who seek to uncover the past.

CHAPTER 3:
URBAN PLANNING AND ARCHITECTURE

Introduction

The genius of the Indus Valley Civilization is perhaps best demonstrated not by its grand monuments or elaborate writings, but by the sheer sophistication of its urban planning and architecture. Cities like Mohenjo-Daro and Harappa showcase a level of civic engineering and urban organization thousands of years ahead. This chapter explores the layout, infrastructure, residential planning, public buildings, and the architectural ingenuity that formed the backbone of this ancient society.

1. A Grid Before Its Time

One of the most remarkable aspects of Indus cities is their grid-based layout. Long before the formal codification of geometry or town planning, the people of Mohenjo-Daro employed a rectilinear street system where roads intersected at right angles, forming a perfect grid of blocks. Main streets were wide, straight, and often flanked by side lanes of uniform width.

This type of urban design, more commonly associated with later civilizations such as the Romans, suggests an advanced understanding of urban geometry and possibly even some form of centralized control or planning authority. The level of symmetry and standardization points to a well-organized bureaucracy capable of overseeing large-scale civic projects.

Streets were not merely thoroughfares; they served as arteries of public life, facilitating trade, transport, and community interaction, all while maintaining hygienic conditions through thoughtful drainage integration.

2. Drainage and Sanitation Systems

Perhaps the most revolutionary aspect of Indus architecture was its emphasis on public sanitation. Every major city, especially Mohenjo-Daro, featured a complex, covered drainage system that ran along the length of the main roads.

Each house was connected to the drainage system via private channels, and drains were built from precisely laid bricks and covered with stone slabs. Maintenance holes and inspection shafts were regularly spaced for cleaning and maintenance.

Homes were equipped with private bathing areas and toilets, an extraordinary feature for a civilization of that era. Household wastewater was channeled into covered drains outside the city walls or soak pits. This meticulous attention to hygiene reflects a civic culture deeply invested in public health and cleanliness.

Even modern planners marvel at the efficiency and foresight of this ancient system, making it one of the earliest known examples of a functional urban sanitation network.

3. Residential Architecture

Houses in Indus Valley cities were typically two-storied, built using standardized, kiln-baked mud bricks. Residences ranged from modest single-room homes to large, multi-roomed structures with central courtyards.

While social hierarchy might be inferred from the size and complexity of homes, the general uniformity in materials and access to amenities such as water and sanitation points toward a relatively egalitarian society.

Most houses were built inward-facing, often with no street-facing windows, a feature that provided both privacy and protection from heat and dust. Rooms were arranged around an open-air courtyard, which likely served as a space for family activities and ventilation.

Doors and staircases were strategically placed, and covered storage areas and underground drains show attention to functionality and comfort. Private wells within some homes further suggest a high value placed on self-sufficiency and convenience.

4. Public Structures and Civic Buildings

Beyond residences, Indus Valley cities boasted impressive public buildings that served civic, religious, or administrative purposes. The most iconic among these is Mohenjo-Daro's Great Bath, a massive, watertight structure measuring approximately 12 meters long, 7 meters wide, and 2.4 meters deep.

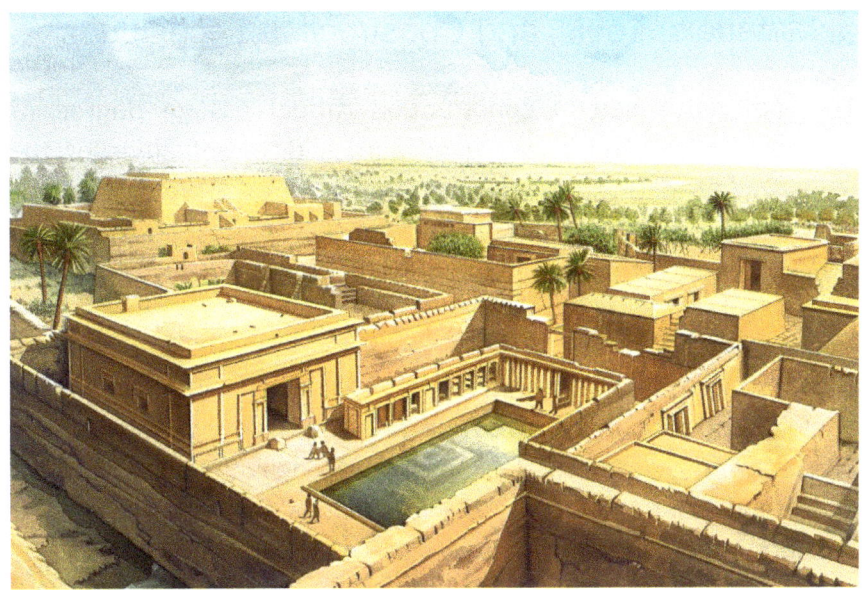

Constructed with finely fitted bricks and a sophisticated waterproofing technique using bitumen, the Great Bath is thought to have been used for ritual bathing or public ceremonies. Small rooms and an adjacent well surround it, suggesting careful water management and public gathering coordination.

Nearby granaries, with ventilated platforms and wide corridors, indicate the existence of central food storage and distribution systems. Such structures hint at a form of economic organization and possibly a governing body that managed communal resources.

Significant buildings, like assembly halls or elevated platforms, may have been administrative centers or marketplaces where the city's social and political life converged.

5. Materials, Tools, and Construction Techniques

The materials used in construction reflect a high degree of standardization. The bricks used across different cities of the Indus Valley followed a near-uniform ratio of 4:2:1 in dimensions (length:width: height). This level of precision suggests using molds and a shared building code, possibly enforced by a central authority.

Construction materials primarily included baked and sun-dried bricks, wood for doors and roofing, and bitumen for waterproofing. These buildings' structural strength and longevity, many of which still stand after thousands of years, speak volumes about their builders' engineering prowess.

The tools used for construction and measurement were simple but effective: plumb bobs, copper saws, chisels, and possibly standardized weights and measuring rods. Even without monumental architecture like pyramids or ziggurats, the cities' functionality and resilience are enduring.

The Indus Valley Civilization's urban planning and architectural brilliance were no accident. It was the product of thoughtful design, social organization, and technological skill. Unlike other ancient civilizations focused on palatial grandeur or religious monuments, the Indus built cities prioritizing public welfare, sustainability, and civic order.

Their cities were clean, well-structured, and efficient, principles that continue to guide modern urban planning. Mohenjo-Daro and its sister cities remind us that the essence of great architecture lies not just in how it looks, but in how it serves its people. Long before modern terms like "infrastructure" and "urbanism" were coined, the builders of the Indus Valley had already laid their foundations.

CHAPTER 4:
DAILY LIFE IN MOHENJO-DARO

Introduction

To truly understand a civilization, one must move beyond its monuments and streets and look into the lives of its people, how they lived, what they wore, ate, believed in, and interacted with their environment and each other. In Mohenjo-Daro, part of the Indus Valley Civilization, the rhythm of daily life was shaped by practical design, social harmony, and a keen sensitivity to nature. Drawing on archaeological finds and interpretive evidence, this chapter offers a glimpse into the everyday existence of the people who called this ancient city home nearly 4,500 years ago.

1. Society and Social Structure

Life in Mohenjo-Daro was likely communal and organized, though not rigidly hierarchical like in many other ancient civilizations. Unlike the grand palaces of Mesopotamia or the monumental tombs of Egypt, Mohenjo-Daro had no evident signs of royalty or vast inequality. Instead, the uniformity in housing, sanitation, and urban access suggests a balanced social fabric with shared civic responsibilities.

There may have been distinctions based on profession, wealth, or

roles in administration or religion, but these divisions were subtle. Artifacts such as elaborate jewelry, finer pottery, and larger homes hint at prosperous households. Yet, the presence of well-built homes for the general populace indicates broad access to resources and urban amenities.

The society likely functioned under the guidance of local administrators or priestly figures, possibly responsible for managing trade, food distribution, religious activities, and civic planning. However, much of the social hierarchy remains speculative without deciphered written records.

2. Homes and Family Life

A typical home in Mohenjo-Daro was designed for both comfort and privacy. Built of baked bricks, homes usually opened into interior courtyards that served as family activity centers. Cooking, washing, and socializing occurred here, shielded from public view and harsh sunlight.

Rooms were arranged around these courtyards and often included sleeping quarters, kitchens, storage areas, and in some cases, private wells and bathrooms. Some homes had second stories, connected by wooden or brick staircases. Floors were made of packed earth or bricks, while ceilings were likely flat and made from wooden beams and clay.

Household life probably revolved around extended family units, with grandparents, parents, and children living under the same roof. The domestic environment emphasized self-sufficiency, with many homes featuring built-in grain bins and access to water, minimizing reliance on communal facilities.

3. Food, Farming, and Diet

Food in Mohenjo-Daro was diverse, nutritious, and primarily locally sourced, though long-distance trade also introduced exotic items. The nearby Indus River and seasonal monsoons supported agriculture, while the fertile alluvial plains allowed the cultivation of wheat, barley, lentils, sesame, mustard, and fruits such as dates and melons.

Cattle, sheep, goats, and poultry were commonly domesticated, and milk, meat, and eggs likely formed part of the diet. Fish and shellfish from the Indus River provided a rich source of protein, as did legumes. Grains were ground using stone querns, and food was likely cooked in clay ovens or over open fires.

Vessels and cooking pots found at the site suggest that food preparation and storage were methodical. Meals were probably hearty but straightforward, consumed from terracotta bowls or metal plates. Some evidence points to communal feasting or food rituals, especially in larger residences or public structures.

4. Clothing and Personal Adornment

While no textiles have survived due to decomposition, figurines, seals, and sculptures offer clues about clothing and fashion in Mohenjo-Daro. Men are typically depicted wearing short robes or loincloths, while women wear longer skirts and possibly shawls draped over the shoulders.

Ornamentation played a significant role in personal appearance. Jewelry made from gold, silver, copper, carnelian, lapis lazuli, and shell was worn by both genders, indicating aesthetic sensibilities and trade connections with regions as far as Mesopotamia and Afghanistan.

Combs, mirrors, and toiletry items suggest that grooming was essential daily. Hairstyles were styled and maintained carelessly; some figurines even show elaborate hair buns and headdresses. Such details reflect a culture that valued cleanliness, beauty, and individuality.

5. Occupations, Crafts, and Trades

The people of Mohenjo-Daro engaged in a wide range of occupations. Farmers, artisans, traders, builders, and laborers formed the foundation of the city's economy. Specialization of labor is evident in the production of standardized weights and measures, beads, ceramics, tools, and metal objects.

Craftspeople worked in workshops or homes, producing pottery, spinning thread, and carving intricate seals that may have served as identification marks or trade tags. The city was a hub of commercial activity, with evidence of local markets and international trade networks.

Seals, marine shells, and semi-precious stones suggest trade with Mesopotamia, the Persian Gulf, and Central Asia. Boats and carts were likely used for transportation, while dockyards or trading posts may have existed along the Indus River, facilitating the exchange of goods and ideas.

6. Religion, Rituals, and Beliefs

Though the precise religious practices of Mohenjo-Daro remain unclear, artifacts hint at a culture rich in spiritual symbolism and possibly ritualistic practices.

Though debated in its function, the famous "Priest-King" statue is thought to depict a religious or noble figure. Terracotta figurines of women interpreted by some as mother goddesses suggest fertility worship. Seals featuring horned animals, trees, and meditative postures indicate connections to nature, animals, and proto-Hindu beliefs.

The Great Bath, one of the most prominent structures in the city, points to ritual bathing or purification ceremonies, reinforcing the cultural importance of cleanliness and spiritual well-being.

Though temples or shrines have not been definitively identified, altars and ritual items found in homes suggest that religious life may have been personal and domestic, rather than centered around large public worship.

7. Recreation and Leisure

Despite their industrious nature, the people of Mohenjo-Daro also made time for recreation and relaxation. Numerous artifacts show signs of leisure activities, such as dice, game boards, and carved toys like miniature carts and animal figurines.

Children likely played with clay figurines, spinning tops, and marbles, while adults may have engaged in board games or music. Small instruments, such as whistles and drums, have been found, suggesting that music and entertainment were a part of social life.

Public spaces like courtyards and platforms might have served as gathering spots for storytelling, community discussions, or festivals. Artifacts showing dancing figures hint at performance arts, possibly linked to seasonal or religious celebrations.

Conclusion

Daily life in Mohenjo-Daro was defined by a balance between function and beauty, private and communal living, work and leisure, ritual and routine. The city's advanced infrastructure supported a self-reliant, organized, and culturally vibrant population. Although many mysteries remain, what emerges from

the ruins is a picture of a society that valued dignity, craftsmanship, hygiene, and harmony.

In the quiet streets and the courtyards of brick houses, we find echoes of laughter, the rhythms of trade, the scent of cooking fires, and the whispered prayers of a people who lived not just in survival, but in refined coexistence with their environment and one another.

CHAPTER 5:
RELIGION AND RITUAL

Introduction

Among the enduring enigmas of the Indus Valley Civilization is its religious life. Unlike other ancient cultures whose gods, temples, and myths are etched in stone or parchment, the people of Mohenjo-Daro and its sister cities left behind no deciphered texts or grand temples. Yet, through art, architecture, and ritual objects, they offered silent but evocative clues into their spiritual worldview. This chapter explores the complex and often symbolic world of religion and ritual practices in Mohenjo-Daro. In this realm, earth, water, fertility, and perhaps even proto-divine figures held sway over the hearts and habits of the people.

1. Clues from the Material World

Without written scriptures or dedicated religious structures, archaeologists have turned to indirect evidence to reconstruct the spiritual beliefs of Mohenjo-Daro's inhabitants. Seals, statues, figurines, altars, amulets, and ceremonial objects provide glimpses of a belief system deeply embedded in everyday life rather than centralized in monumental institutions.

The absence of prominent temples or shrines suggests that religion may have been personal, localized, or household-based, with rituals performed in homes, courtyards, or open public platforms. This decentralized approach indicates that spirituality was woven into the fabric of daily life rather than confined to elite priesthoods or royal mandates.

2. The Great Bath: Ritual and Purification

The Great Bath of Mohenjo-Daro is the most striking evidence for religious or ceremonial activity. This large, rectangular pool, expertly constructed with watertight brickwork and surrounded by a colonnade, is widely believed to have been used for ritual bathing or purification ceremonies.

Water, a universal symbol of purity and rebirth, may have played a central role in the spiritual life of the Indus. Individuals might have immersed themselves before ceremonies, seasonal festivals, or as part of personal penance. Its placement within a public building and proximity to smaller changing rooms suggest organized, possibly communal, ritual activity.

The Great Bath's sophistication, including a drainage system, stairs, and an adjacent well, implies its cultural and spiritual significance. While no inscriptions clarify its use, scholars widely agree that it was a sacred space, marking the intersection of public life and private devotion.

3. Seals and Symbols: Pantheon or Principles?

Thousands of steatite seals recovered from Mohenjo-Daro depict many motifs, many of which are believed to hold religious or cosmological meaning. Among the most iconic is the image of a seated figure surrounded by animals, popularly known as the "Proto-Shiva" or Pashupati seal.

This figure, seated in a yogic posture with horns or a headdress, resembles later depictions of the Hindu god Shiva as Lord of Beasts (Pashupati). If the connection holds, it would suggest that aspects of Hinduism have roots in Indus traditions.

Other seals depict sacred animals, bulls, elephants, rhinoceroses, and unicorn-like creatures, possibly as totemic symbols or divine avatars. The repetition and careful carving of these symbols suggest they carried ritual or protective value, perhaps invoking strength, fertility, or guidance.

Still, whether these were literal deities, spiritual concepts, or clan emblems remains unknown. These images were deliberately chosen, often worn or stamped, and held deep symbolic weight for those who used them.

4. The Mother Goddess and Fertility Worship

One of the most debated artifacts of the Indus civilization is the terracotta figurine of a female figure, often referred to as the Mother Goddess. These statues, found in multiple forms and sizes, frequently depict a woman with exaggerated reproductive features, adorned with jewelry and elaborate headgear.

These figures may have been associated with fertility rites, agricultural cycles, or goddess worship, similar to practices seen in prehistoric Europe, Mesopotamia, and later Vedic culture. Their widespread presence suggests that reverence for the female principle, giver of life and nurturer of land, was central to Indus spirituality.

Such figurines may have been household idols, used in domestic rituals to ensure healthy offspring, successful harvests, or protection from disease. They point to a worldview that honored earthly cycles, creation, and regeneration themes deeply embedded in agrarian societies.

5. Sacred Animals and Symbolic Beasts

Animal reverence played a prominent role in Mohenjo-Daro's spiritual landscape. The humped bull, often depicted on seals, is believed to symbolize power, virility, and endurance. Bulls may have been associated with masculine strength or divine protectors.

The unicorn-like creature, an animal with a single horn, often shown near ritual altars, has no known real-world equivalent. It may represent a mythical being or spiritual guardian, but its significance is lost to time.

Other sacred animals include:

- Elephants – wisdom and strength
- Tigers and leopards – danger, divinity, or spiritual trials
- Fish and birds – life, fertility, or transitions between realms

The regularity with which these animals appear, often in stylized, symmetrical forms, suggests they were not just artistic motifs but sacred emblems, each with spiritual or ritualistic meaning.

6. Ritual Objects and Domestic Worship

Aside from figurines and seals, archaeologists have uncovered altars, incense burners, amulets, and miniature tools that appear to have been used in ritual contexts. Some homes had small niches in the walls or dedicated platforms, suggesting the existence of domestic shrines.

The use of fire altars or ritual hearths, though more common in Harappan outposts like Kalibangan, points to the possibility of fire-based ceremonies involving offerings or purification.

Amulets and pendants found in burials or worn as jewelry may have served as protective charms, imbued with symbolic meaning or spiritual power. Clay tablets with geometric patterns may have been used in divination, meditation, or sacred geometry.

Rituals likely included food, incense, water, or light offerings, all consistent with agrarian spiritual traditions that sought balance between nature, ancestors, and the divine.

7. Life After Death: Burial Practices and Beliefs

Burial customs provide further insight into Indus beliefs about death and the afterlife. Graves at Mohenjo-Daro were typically simple pits, sometimes lined with bricks, where the body was laid out with personal belongings, pottery, ornaments, and food offerings.

The presence of grave goods implies a belief in an existence beyond death, where the deceased might require sustenance, tools, or spiritual protection. Yet, compared to contemporaneous civilizations, the absence of grand tombs or mummification rituals suggests a pragmatic, humble attitude toward death.

Children, adults, and elderly individuals were buried in different types of graves, possibly reflecting stages of life or beliefs about the soul's journey. While not dominant, cremation may have also been practiced in certain regions.

Whether the Indus people believed in reincarnation, ancestral spirits, or heavenly realms is unknown, but the care and intention behind burials point to a culture deeply invested in spiritual continuity.

Conclusion

Religion and ritual in Mohenjo-Daro were intimate, symbolic, and deeply entwined with nature and daily life. In a civilization without ziggurats or cathedrals, the sacred was found in water, animals, fertility, and the quiet spaces of the home.

Though the specifics of their belief system remain veiled, the archaeological record reveals a people who sought harmony with the cosmos, honored the cycles of life and death, and infused their world with meaning beyond the material.

Their gods may be unnamed, and their prayers unheard, but the rituals of Mohenjo-Daro endure etched in clay, shaped by hand, and immortalized in the sacred geometry of their city.

CHAPTER 6:
TRADE AND ECONOMY

Introduction

The economic vitality of a civilization reveals much about its people, how they sustained themselves, interacted with neighbors, and adapted to changing landscapes. In the case of Mohenjo-Daro, the archaeological evidence paints a picture of a thriving urban economy grounded in agriculture, craftsmanship, and robust trade networks. The city's success was not accidental but the result of careful planning, resource management, and a remarkable capacity for commerce both within the Indus Valley and with far-flung regions of Mesopotamia, Central Asia, and beyond.

This chapter delves into the economic life of Mohenjo-Daro, from its production systems and artisanal industries to its extensive trade connections and the administrative tools that may have sustained its prosperity.

1. An Agrarian Foundation

At the heart of Mohenjo-Daro's economy was agriculture. Fertile soil, seasonal flooding from the Indus River, and advanced irrigation supported the cultivation of staple crops such as:

- Wheat and barley – the region's primary grains

- Millet, lentils, and peas – important protein sources

- Cotton – one of the earliest known examples of cotton cultivation in human history

- Sesame and mustard seeds – used for oil and seasoning

- Fruits like dates, melons, and pomegranates

Farming was likely done in fields outside the city, with seasonal patterns governed by the monsoon. Oxen and water buffalo helped plow fields, and granaries stored surplus harvests. The large granary near the citadel suggests that grain collection may have been centrally organized, possibly through a taxation or redistribution system.

Agriculture sustained the population and created surpluses that enabled trade and urban specialization.

2. Skilled Artisans and Urban Production

Mohenjo-Daro was a hub of artisanal excellence, producing high-quality goods using locally sourced and imported materials. Evidence of workshops, kilns, bead-making centers, and tool production has been uncovered in various parts of the city.

Key industries included:

- Pottery: Durable and artistically crafted vessels, often decorated with geometric motifs

- Bead-making: A flourishing craft using carnelian, agate, shell, and steatite to produce intricate necklaces and bangles

- Textiles: Though no fabric survives, spindle whorls and loom weights point to a significant cotton and wool industry

- Metalworking: Use of copper, bronze, and occasionally gold to create tools, weapons, and ornaments

- Shell carving: Crafting of decorative items from marine shells, often traded over long distances

Artisans likely lived in close-knit communities, and their goods formed the backbone of Mohenjo-Daro's domestic market and international exports.

3. Internal Trade and Marketplaces

The economic infrastructure of Mohenjo-Daro was designed to support urban commerce and market activity. While no formal market squares have been discovered, the wide streets, shopfronts, and storage facilities suggest that trade occurred throughout the city, possibly in open courtyards, along main thoroughfares, or in specialized zones.

Goods traded internally may have included:

- Food and spices
- Tools and implements
- Textiles and garments
- Ritual or decorative items
- Firewood and building materials

Standardized weights and measures, many found in homes and public buildings, point to regulated economic transactions. The consistency of these weights based on binary multiples (e.g., 1, 2, 4, 8) suggests a sophisticated understanding of accounting and fairness in trade.

Some scholars believe the Indus may have used tokens or seals to mark ownership or authorize trade, functioning like early trademarks or identification labels.

4. Long-Distance Trade Networks

Perhaps the most fascinating aspect of Mohenjo-Daro's economy is its extensive external trade. The city was part of a vast commercial web that stretched from the mountains of Afghanistan to the ports of the Persian Gulf, and even into the heart of Mesopotamia.

Primary trade links included:

- Mesopotamia (modern-day Iraq): Indus seals have been found in cities like Ur and Sumer, indicating a strong exchange relationship. Mesopotamian texts refer to "Meluhha", widely believed to be the Indus Valley.

- Oman and Bahrain: Marine shells and copper ingots point to active maritime trade with the Arabian Peninsula.

- Afghanistan and Baluchistan: Provided lapis lazuli, turquoise, and tin.

- Gujarat and Rajasthan: Inland trade brought semi-precious stones, salt, and minerals.

Exports likely included beads, textiles, wood, ivory, metalwork, cotton, and grains. In return, Mohenjo-Daro imported luxury goods, metals, and exotic stones, incorporated into local crafts or rituals.

Trade was conducted via rivers, land caravans, and seafaring boats, with Mohenjo-Daro's location near the lower Indus making it an ideal distribution center.

5. Tools of Commerce: Weights, Seals, and Administration

An organized bureaucracy or guild-based structure likely supported the economic system of Mohenjo-Daro. Evidence of this comes from:

- Stone weights: Carefully calibrated, cube-shaped weights suggest standardized commercial transactions. These were essential for fair trade and taxation.

- Seals: Used for marking goods, identifying merchants, or

authorizing transactions. Some were inscribed with pictographic symbols, possibly indicating names, commodities, or origin.

- Granaries and storage rooms: Centralized grain collection implies resource management on a civic scale, potentially for redistribution during droughts, festivals, or military needs.

Although the Indus script remains undeciphered, consistent symbols across cities suggest a shared economic language that helped regulate and facilitate trade.

6. Currency and Medium of Exchange

Unlike Mesopotamia or Egypt, there is no evidence of coins or formal currency in Mohenjo-Daro. Trade likely operated on a barter system or was supported by commodity-based exchange, such as:

- Grains or metal ingots as standardized trade values

- Use of weights and measures to equate value

- Seals as proof of ownership or authorization

The lack of coinage does not indicate a lack of sophistication. On the contrary, the Indus system was likely adapted to suit local and regional trade, ensuring fair transactions through tangible value rather than minted currency.

7. Economic Organization and Urban Wealth

The consistent urban design across the Indus cities, including Mohenjo-Daro, Harappa, and Dholavira, points to a shared economic model and possibly a centralized or federated administrative system. Whether ruled by priest-kings, councils, or merchant guilds, Mohenjo-Daro's economy required:

- Efficient food storage and distribution
- Oversight of production standards
- Regulation of trade routes and taxes
- Maintenance of infrastructure and labor coordination

Public works such as roads, drains, and wells indicate collective investment, perhaps funded by grain levies or labor taxes.

Despite the lack of palaces or treasuries, Mohenjo-Daro exhibits signs of widespread prosperity and civic wealth evenly distributed rather than concentrated in elite hands. This may reflect an egalitarian economic philosophy, with surplus wealth reinvested into public goods.

Conclusion

A remarkable fusion of agriculture, artisanal skill, and international trade drove the economic engine of Mohenjo-Daro. It was a city not of kings and conquests, but of craftspeople, traders, and administrators, all working in tandem within a sophisticated and stable economic framework.

Through its markets and workshops, seals and weights, long-distance caravans, and coastal docks, Mohenjo-Daro stands as a testament to the power of peaceful commerce. This civilization chose prosperity over conquest and collaboration over coercion.

Its economic legacy, silent yet resilient, continues to inspire admiration and inquiry, a forgotten metropolis that thrived not just in stone and brick but in the art of exchange.

CHAPTER 7:
ART, CRAFTS, AND CULTURE

Introduction

The city of Mohenjo-Daro was more than a marvel of urban planning and trade; it was a vibrant cultural center alive with artistic expression, craftsmanship, and refined aesthetics. Though the Indus Valley Civilization lacked towering monuments or decipherable literary texts, its art speaks volumes quietly, revealing a society that valued beauty, balance, symbolism, and technical skill.

This chapter explores the artistic and cultural life of Mohenjo-Daro, a civilization whose creativity continues to captivate scholars and art lovers alike, from intricate beadwork to enigmatic seals, from terracotta figurines to the subtle elegance of painted pottery.

1. Art as a Reflection of Life

Art in Mohenjo-Daro wasn't created for spectacle alone. It was functional, symbolic, and deeply woven into the rhythm of everyday life. Whether etched on a seal, molded in clay, or painted onto pottery, artistic expression served spiritual, decorative, commercial, and personal purposes.

Indus artisans worked with a variety of materials, including:

- Clay and terracotta
- Steatite (a soft stone)
- Shell, ivory, and bone
- Copper and bronze
- Semi-precious
- Stones like carnelian, lapis lazuli, and agate

The craftsmanship and aesthetic coherence across Mohenjo-Daro's artifacts indicate a shared cultural identity and an appreciation for beauty, order, and precision.

2. Seals: Symbolic and Sophisticated

Perhaps the most iconic artistic artifacts of the Indus Valley are the steatite seals, small, square plaques intricately carved with animal motifs, mythic creatures, and undeciphered script. Thousands have been discovered in Mohenjo-Daro, serving both practical and symbolic roles.

Features of the seals:

- Typically 2–4 cm square, made of fired steatite

- Engraved with animals like bulls, elephants, unicorns, and composite beasts

- Accompanied by short inscriptions in the Indus script

- Often had a boss or hole at the back, allowing them to be worn or stamped

Their exact use remains debated: they may have marked property, identified merchants, authorized trade, or held ritual power. The sheer artistry of the engravings, detailed even on such a small scale, showcases Indus artists' technical brilliance and abstract imagination.

3. Terracotta Figurines: The Human Form and Beyond

Terracotta figurines provide a more personal and domestic glimpse into the cultural life of Mohenjo-Daro. These miniature clay sculptures, often found in homes, are thought to have served religious, decorative, or playful functions.

Common figurine types:

- The so-called "Mother Goddess" figures with exaggerated feminine features, possibly used in fertility rituals
- Male figures adorned with jewelry or headdresses, occasionally with animal traits
- Animals such as bulls, birds, dogs, and monkeys
- Toys, including miniature carts, rattles, and spinning tops, some with movable parts

These figurines reflect daily life, beliefs, and relationships, capturing Indus culture's sacred, whimsical, and familial aspects.

4. Beadwork and Jewelry: Personal Adornment

Jewelry in Mohenjo-Daro was not merely ornamental; it signified status, identity, and cultural refinement. Indus artisans produced a vast array of personal adornments, including:

- Beads made of carnelian, agate, faience, and lapis lazuli

- Earrings, bangles, pendants, and necklaces

- Metal ornaments of copper, bronze, and occasionally gold

- Shell bracelets and carved bangles, found primarily in female graves

The bead-making industry in Mohenjo-Daro was particularly advanced. Artisans used drills, polishing stones, and furnaces to create beads precisely. Some carnelian beads display etched patterns, achieved through a complex bleaching technique that speaks to high levels of chemical knowledge.

Jewelry was worn by men, women, and children alike, suggesting a culture where aesthetic expression was accessible to all.

5. Pottery and Painted Ware

Mohenjo-Daro's pottery, abundant across the site, reflects a blend of utility and elegance. Most vessels were wheel-thrown and fired in kilns, ranging from simple storage jars to finely painted ceremonial wares.

Styles and motifs:

- Geometric designs: circles, lines, chevrons, and zigzags
- Floral and faunal motifs: peacocks, fish, pipal leaves
- Red slip and black paint, giving a distinctive contrast

The uniformity in shape and decoration suggests standardization and aesthetic continuity, while regional variations hint at local artistic schools or guilds. Many vessels were likely used for storing grains, liquids, and offerings, merging beauty with function.

6. Sculptures in Stone and Bronze

Although rare, larger sculptures from Mohenjo-Daro exhibit remarkable realism and elegance. The most famous example is the "Priest-King" statue:

- A 17.5 cm tall bust made of white steatite

- Draped in a patterned robe, with a headband and calm, introspective expression

- Possibly a religious leader, nobleman, or symbolic figure of authority

Equally famous is the bronze "Dancing Girl":

- A 10.5 cm tall metal sculpture of a young girl with a confident posture

- Right hand on hip, left arm adorned with bangles

- Suggests that movement, rhythm, and self-awareness are extraordinary qualities for Bronze Age art

These masterpieces show that Indus artists had a keen eye for human anatomy, proportion, and expression, rivaling the works of contemporary civilizations.

7. Cultural Symbolism and Everyday Aesthetics

Beyond objects of art, the culture of Mohenjo-Daro expressed itself in urban form, attire, personal grooming, and symbolic motifs. Art was not confined to elite spaces; it permeated public life, private homes, and daily customs.

Cultural elements included:

- Cosmetics and grooming items: combs, mirrors, and kohl containers

- Decorated bricks and tiles: Some buildings had aesthetic embellishments

- Musical instruments: terracotta rattles and flutes indicate musical traditions

- Board games and dice: suggesting recreational and possibly ritualistic activities

Symbolism was central to Indus culture. The repeated use of motifs, such as trees, horned animals, and circular patterns, likely held cosmic, seasonal, or spiritual meaning. The pipal tree, for instance, appears in several contexts and may have been revered, foreshadowing its later sacred status in Hinduism and Buddhism.

8. Cultural Unity and Artistic Legacy

One of Mohenjo-Daro's most striking cultural features is the Indus region's unity. Similar artistic styles, motifs, and techniques appear in Harappa, Dholavira, Lothal, and other Indus cities, pointing to shared traditions and possibly cultural exchanges.

Despite their decline, the artistic traditions of the Indus Valley may have influenced later South Asian cultures. Symbols, techniques, and creative themes reappear in early Vedic art, Hindu iconography, and folk crafts, a quiet thread of continuity that speaks to the enduring soul of this lost civilization.

Conclusion

Mohenjo-Daro was not just a city of engineers and traders; it was a city of artists, makers, and cultural thinkers. Its people channeled their creativity into grand and humble objects, shaping a material culture that balanced utility and beauty, ritual and realism, tradition and innovation.

Though time has erased their names and silenced their songs, the legacy of Indus art and culture lives on in the grace of a terracotta dancer, in the curve of a painted pot, in the enduring mystery of a seal. Mohenjo-Daro remains, in every sense, a civilization of the imagination.

CHAPTER 8: THE ENIGMA OF THE INDUS SCRIPT

Introduction

None of the many mysteries surrounding the Indus Valley Civilization is as haunting—or intellectually tantalizing-as as its undeciphered script. The Indus script is one of the world's last great undecoded writing systems, carved into seals, etched on pottery, and inscribed on tools. It can unlock answers about governance, religion, economy, and language—perhaps even names of kings, cities, or gods.

Yet despite over a century of research, the script remains silent and enigmatic. It is as if Mohenjo-Daro and its sister cities are whispering from the depths of time, but in a language we no longer understand.

In this chapter, we explore the known facts about the Indus script, the nature of its symbols, its possible functions, and the major theories that attempt to unravel its secrets.

1. Discovery and Distribution

The first known examples of the Indus script were discovered during the early 20th-century excavations at Harappa and Mohenjo-Daro. From the beginning, archaeologists recognized that these tiny symbols bore the hallmarks of a writing system, yet they differed radically from known scripts of the ancient world.

Key facts:

- Over 4,000 inscribed artifacts have been found, mostly seals, pottery, tools, and tablets

- The script appears in urban centers, workshops, and trade contexts

- Symbols are typically incised or carved, rarely painted

- The majority of inscriptions are very short, averaging 4–5 signs in length, though a few contain up to 17 characters

The distribution of the script across a vast territory—from northern Afghanistan to Gujarat—demonstrates a shared linguistic or administrative system, possibly linked to commerce, identity, or religious rituals.

2. Structure and Features of the Script

The Indus script consists of over 400 unique signs, many of which appear to be composite or symbolic. Some signs resemble abstract shapes, while others depict animals, plants, or human figures.

Distinctive features include:

- Pictographic elements, such as fish, birds, human forms, and tools

- Geometric patterns: including circles, lines, tridents, and loops

- Directionality: Most inscriptions are written from right to left

- No spaces or punctuation, though signs often appear in clusters or groupings

- Sign repetition and positional rules suggest a formal grammar or syntax.

The signs seem highly stylized, pointing toward a mature and sophisticated system, possibly developed over centuries.

3. Script or Symbol System?

One of the primary debates among scholars is whether the Indus script constitutes a proper writing system or a more limited proto-script or symbol system.

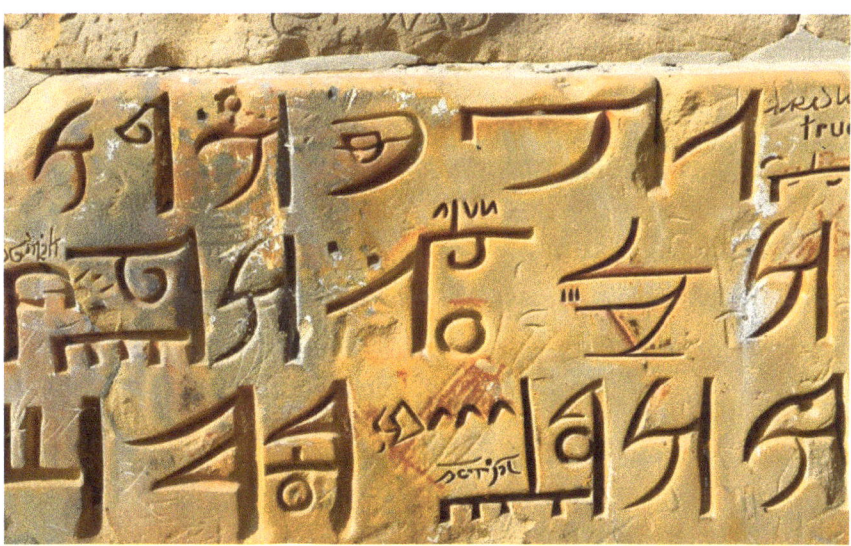

- Supporters of the "true script" theory argue that the signs represent a fully developed writing system, possibly logographic, syllabic, or a mix, similar to Sumerian cuneiform or Egyptian hieroglyphs.

- Skeptics argue that the brevity of inscriptions and lack of longer texts suggest the signs function more like emblems or trade marks, used to identify goods, families, or deities.

Recent computational analyses have shown statistical patterns similar to known writing systems, lending weight to the idea that it was a structured form of communication.

4. Attempts at Decipherment

Over the decades, scholars, linguists, mathematicians, and cryptographers have proposed dozens of decipherments. However, none have achieved consensus.

Major hypotheses:

- Dravidian Hypothesis: One of the most widely supported theories—championed by scholars like Iravatham Mahadevan—suggests the script encodes an early form of Proto-Dravidian, the ancestral language of Tamil and other South Indian tongues.

- Indo-Aryan Hypothesis: Proposes links to early Vedic Sanskrit, though most scholars now view this as chronologically implausible.

- Munda or Austroasiatic Theory: Suggests links with the languages of eastern India, such as Santali or Mundari.

- Structural Analysis and AI Models: Recent efforts have used machine learning and statistical modeling to identify repeating sign patterns, grammatical rules, and positional logic—some promising correlations, but no definitive breakthrough.

All attempts are handicapped by the lack of a Rosetta Stone—a bilingual inscription that could link the Indus script to a known language.

5. Contexts and Possible Functions

Though we cannot read the inscriptions, we can analyze their contexts to infer potential purposes.

Common uses:

- Seals and sealings: Possibly used for stamping ownership, authenticating goods, or identifying merchants and families.

- Pottery marks: May indicate contents, owner, or production origin.

- Miniature tablets: Could have been used for accounting, tallying, or ceremonial purposes.

- Amulets and ritual objects: Suggest religious or magical significance.

The consistency of sign use across locations indicates shared meanings and literacy among elites or traders. It's plausible that only certain classes—administrators, merchants, or priests—were literate.

6. Symbolism and Visual Language

Beyond phonetic content, the Indus script may have had a symbolic or spiritual function. Recurrent motifs—like the unicorn, pipal leaf, or horned deity—hint at a visual language rich in mythological or ritual meaning.

- The "fish" sign, one of the most common, may represent both a literal fish and a phonetic or symbolic idea—possibly "star" or "god," if read through Dravidian roots.

- The "standard device," often placed before animal images, might be a religious emblem or totem.

- Some seals show complex scenes, such as a horned figure surrounded by animals (possibly a proto-Shiva or "Pashupati" figure), suggesting narrative or cosmological intent.

Even if not "read" in a conventional sense, these inscriptions likely communicated ideas and encoded authority, spirituality, or identity.

7. Why Has the Script Not Been Deciphered?

Several unique challenges have prevented the decipherment of the Indus script:

- Short inscriptions: With no long texts, it isn't easy to establish grammatical structure or word boundaries.

- Unknown language: The spoken language behind the script is completely lost.

- No bilingual texts: Unlike the Rosetta Stone for Egyptian, no parallel texts serve as decoding tools.

- Lack of context: Many inscriptions come from ruins without associated artifacts to aid interpretation.

Despite these obstacles, researchers continue to progress by analyzing sign frequencies, regional variations, and possible rebus interpretations.

8. Cultural Significance and Legacy

The Indus script reflects a complex cognitive culture, whether a full-fledged script or a sacred symbolic system. It speaks to a people who valued record-keeping, identity, and perhaps ritual codification. Its influence may even echo in later Indian scripts:

- Sure signs resemble symbols found in early Brahmi, the script used for Ashokan edicts.
- Some motifs, like the trident or svastika, persist in Hindu

and Buddhist symbolism.

- The conceptual legacy of visual communication, sacred geometry, and cosmological mapping may have informed South Asian religious art.

Thus, even in silence, the script connects the ancient Indus world to modern India's cultural and philosophical foundations.

Conclusion

The Indus script remains one of the most fantastic unsolved puzzles of the ancient world—a silent testament to a civilization both intellectually rich and creatively expressive. Its brevity taunts us. Its beauty captivates us. And its mystery invites every new generation of scholars, linguists, and dreamers to imagine the stories locked within.

Perhaps one day, a single seal or inscription will unlock the door to understanding. Until then, the script stands as an elegant enigma, guarding the secrets of a civilization that knew how to build, trade, govern, and speak in symbols that defy time.

CHAPTER NINE: GOVERNANCE AND SOCIAL STRUCTURE

Introduction

One of the most fascinating aspects of Mohenjo-Daro and the wider Indus Valley Civilization is how complex, vast, and meticulously planned cities seem to have functioned without clear evidence of kings, palaces, or monumental temples. This absence of ostentatious rulers or central figures contrasts with contemporary civilizations like Mesopotamia or Egypt, where authority was personified in god-kings and priests.

Yet the society built Mohenjo-Daro exhibited order, coordination, and long-term planning, hinting at a structured governance system and a defined social hierarchy. This chapter explores how power, leadership, and social organization might have worked in a civilization whose silence leaves more to interpretation than record.

1. A City Without Kings?

Unlike the pharaohs of Egypt or the priest-kings of Mesopotamia, the Indus Valley has no surviving statues, inscriptions, or tombs dedicated to rulers or elite individuals. Mohenjo-Daro, for all its architectural grandeur, contains no palaces, royal cemeteries, or murals glorifying leadership.

What does this absence suggest?

- Decentralized authority: Power may have been distributed among councils, local guilds, or urban administrators.

- Collective governance: Leadership could have emerged from community consensus, religious authorities, or trade collectives.

- Symbolic leadership: The figure often called the "Priest-King" may not have been a monarch but a ceremonial or spiritual leader.

This lack of obvious hierarchy in visual culture has led some scholars to label the Indus civilization as "egalitarian", but archaeological evidence suggests a more nuanced picture.

2. Urban Planning as Political Expression

The very structure of Mohenjo-Daro reflects intentionality, regulation, and central oversight—indicators of a capable administrative body.

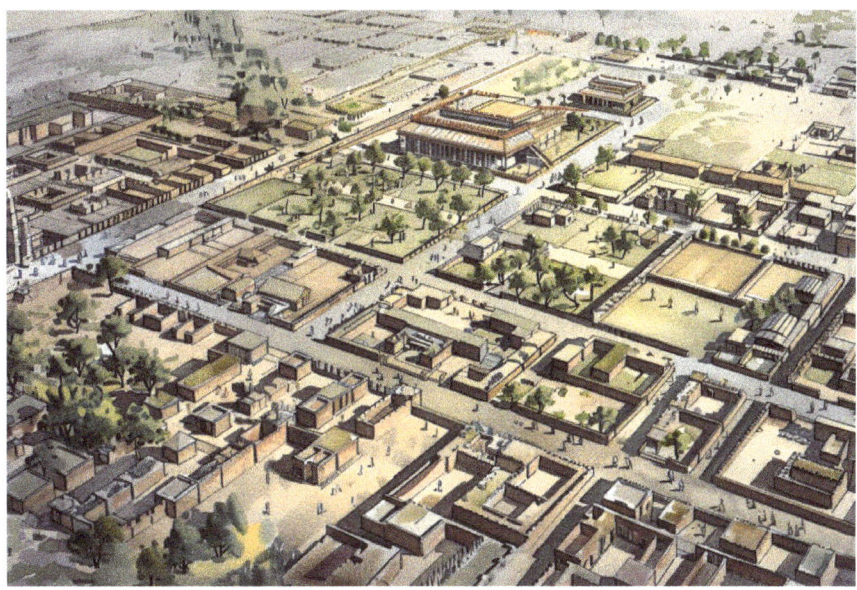

Key elements of coordinated governance:

- Grid-like city planning, with straight streets and standardized block sizes

- Zoning, separating residential, industrial, and administrative sectors

- Centralized granaries and warehouses, likely controlled and rationed by officials

- Standardized weights and measures, vital for trade and taxation

- Sophisticated water management, including public baths, wells, and drainage

Such complexity implies rules, enforcement, and institutional planning. Though the rulers remain anonymous, their influence is etched into the city's bricks.

3. Administrative Structures and Economic Control

The discovery of extensive storage facilities, seal-marked goods, and uniform trade weights points to a bureaucratic structure that oversaw agriculture, trade, and public resources.

Possible administrative systems:

- Merchants' guilds or trade councils: Who regulated commerce and standards?

- Priestly administrators, who may have governed through ritual authority and calendar-based agriculture.

- State officials or scribes: Suggested by the presence of seals and possible inventory systems.

The widespread use of Indus seals suggests a form of administrative control, used to mark ownership, approve transactions, or designate official goods.

It is plausible that a class of literate administrators—perhaps based in centralized buildings like the "Great Granary" or "Assembly Hall"—managed the city's economic and logistical systems.

4. The Social Pyramid: Class and Occupation

Despite limited direct evidence, clues from architecture, burials, and material culture reveal a society with social stratification, even if subtle by ancient standards.

Indicators of social differentiation:

- Varied housing: From large multi-room brick homes with private wells to single-room dwellings.

- Access to luxury goods: Carnelian beads, faience bangles, and metal tools were unevenly distributed.

- Specialized labor: Artisans, metalworkers, beadmakers, and bricklayers show occupational divisions.

- Burial differences: Some graves contain pottery and

ornaments, while others are simple or empty.

Society likely included:

- Elite administrators or the priestly class (possibly those in charge of grain storage, rituals, or regional coordination)

- Merchants and traders

- Artisans and artisans

- Farmers, laborers, and possibly servants

Although no slave class has been identified, labor stratification likely existed, especially given the scale of public works.

5. The Role of Women in Society

The role of women in Mohenjo-Daro is still debated, but archaeological finds suggest a level of visibility and agency in various domains of life.

Key observations:

- Terracotta figurines prominently feature women, often depicted with jewelry or in ritual poses.

- Burial goods found with women include ornaments and tools, indicating respect or ownership.

- The absence of oppressive iconography (like depictions of subjugation) could suggest a relatively equitable social environment.

Though concrete evidence is still lacking, women may have played roles in household economy, craft production, ritual life, and possibly local governance.

6. Law, Order, and Social Conduct

The efficient operation of a massive city like Mohenjo-Daro—without signs of rebellion, fortification, or disorder—hints at a well-maintained law and civil responsibility system.

Although we lack written laws like Hammurabi's Code, the uniformity of civic life suggests:

- Rules for urban conduct, sanitation, and property rights
- Customary laws are potentially enforced by local councils or priestly officials

- Moral codes are possibly tied to religious or ritual beliefs

The near absence of weapons, war imagery, or prisons suggests that social cohesion was maintained through norms, rituals, and mutual dependence rather than coercive violence.

7. Mohenjo-Daro's Place in a Larger Network

Mohenjo-Daro was not an isolated city but part of a larger urban and rural network, including Harappa, Dholavira, Kalibangan, and hundreds of smaller settlements.

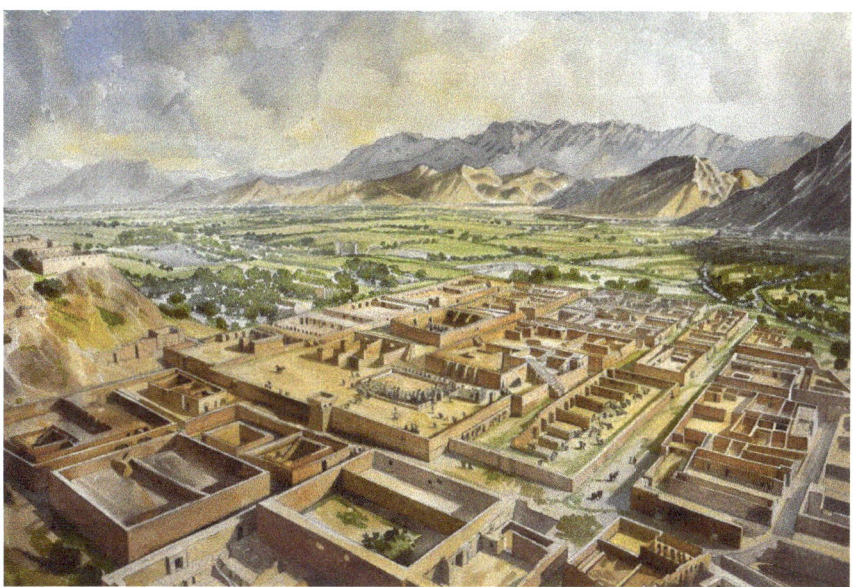

Governance may have operated through a confederation model:

- City-states that shared cultural and economic systems
- A central hub-and-spoke model with regional capitals and local village councils

- Possible ritual centers acting as unifying sites for festivals, trade fairs, or governance councils

Standardized bricks, weights, and seals across the region imply a cohesive yet decentralized authority—a hallmark of stable federated governance.

8. Decline and the Question of Leadership

As the Indus cities began to decline around 1900 BCE, so too may have been the governance structures. Evidence of urban decay, depopulation, and standardization loss suggests a breakdown of the central authority.

Theories include:

- Environmental changes leading to agricultural collapse
- Shifts in trade routes reduce economic strength
- Internal social or political fragmentation

Without monumental rulers or inscriptions, the fall of Mohenjo-Daro is as quietly mysterious as its rise—an egalitarian giant that faded without drama, war, or tyranny.

Conclusion

The social and political systems of Mohenjo-Daro challenge our assumptions about ancient civilizations. In place of emperors and conquests, we find quiet order, collective planning, and sophisticated civic life. It may have been a society where community outweighed kingship, and ritual, trade, and regulation formed the backbone of governance.

Though nameless, the leaders of Mohenjo-Daro shaped a civilization whose influence still echoes. Their legacy lies not in statues or conquests, but in the layout of their streets, the purity of their planning, and the harmony of their urban vision. In this anonymity lies perhaps their most significant achievement: a civilization built not on ego, but on equity, cooperation, and civic wisdom.

CHAPTER TEN: WATER, SANITATION, AND ENGINEERING

Introduction

Few ancient cities astonish modern archaeologists as profoundly as Mohenjo-Daro does in urban engineering, particularly water management and sanitation. Long before the invention of modern plumbing, this Indus Valley metropolis had developed a system of drains, wells, baths, and sewage disposal that rivals many modern standards in both scope and sophistication.

In an era when other civilizations were only beginning to grasp the challenges of urban waste and water supply, Mohenjo-Daro stood as a paragon of hygienic city design, reflecting advanced engineering and a deep cultural commitment to cleanliness, public health, and civic order.

This chapter explores the remarkable water systems of Mohenjo-Daro—its wells, baths, drainage channels, and stormwater management—and considers what these technologies reveal about the civilization's values, ingenuity, and administrative skill.

1. A City Engineered for Water

Mohenjo-Daro's relationship with water was vital and strategic on the Indus River's banks. While the river provided a life source, the city's engineers ensured that water was distributed, stored, and disposed of with precise control and efficiency.

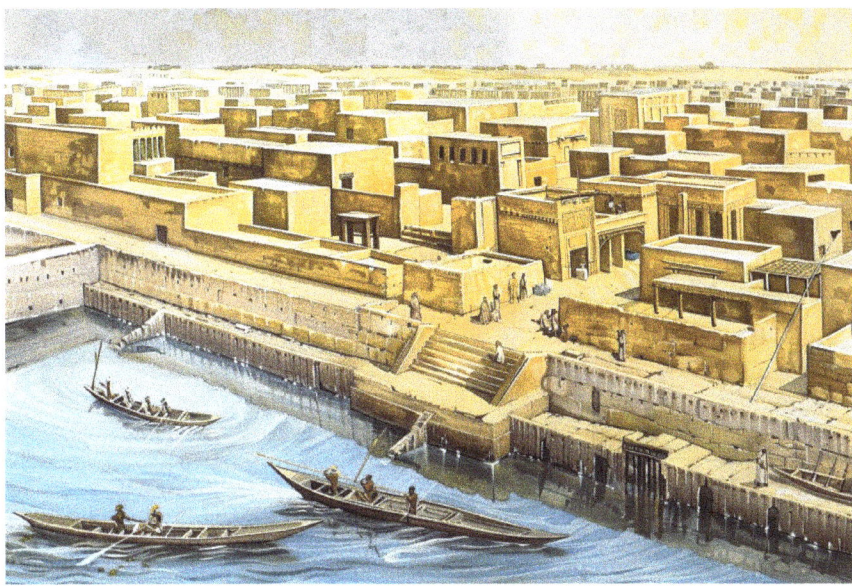

Key statistics:

- Over 700 wells have been discovered within the city's bounds

- Many homes had private bathing areas and toilets

- Drainage systems ran beneath streets and behind buildings

- Water infrastructure was built using uniform baked bricks, ensuring durability and consistency

The prevalence of water-related structures suggests that sanitation was not merely practical—it was integral to the city's cultural and civic identity.

2. The Great Bath: A Civic Masterpiece

Perhaps the most iconic structure in Mohenjo-Daro is the Great Bath, located in the Citadel mound. This rectangular brick-lined pool, measuring approximately 12 meters long, 7 meters wide, and 2.5 meters deep, is widely believed to have held ritual significance.

Architectural features:

- Waterproofing with bitumen along the floor and walls

- Steps leading down into the bath from two sides

- Covered drains to allow for controlled inflow and outflow

of water

- A nearby well, likely the bath's water source
- Changing rooms and platforms surrounding the structure

The Great Bath represents a fusion of architecture, engineering, and cultural practice, whether used for purification, ceremonial bathing, or public gathering.

3. Wells and Water Supply Systems

Wells were a common sight in Mohenjo-Daro—nearly every street or cluster of homes had access to one, and many houses had private wells.

Features of the well systems:

- Built from baked bricks in circular shapes, often tapering toward the bottom
- Connected to platforms or basins for drawing and collecting water
- Some wells were located in public courtyards, serving communal needs
- Several had adjacent staircases, making them easily accessible for women and children

These wells were not simply water sources but daily life centers, enabling cooking, cleaning, bathing, and ritual practices.

4. Private Toilets and Bathing Areas

One of the most astonishing features of Mohenjo-Daro's homes is the presence of indoor sanitation facilities. In an age when most urban societies lacked even the concept of private hygiene, many houses in this city were equipped with bathrooms and toilets.

Common configurations:

- Small bathing platforms, usually made of baked bricks and located in corner rooms
- Toilets constructed as vertical shafts lined with clay rings or bricks
- Waste channeled into covered drains or soak pits
- Water from bathing areas drained directly into the municipal sewer lines

The engineering reflects an intuitive understanding of water flow, gravity, and cleanliness. That so many homes included these features suggests a culture in which hygiene was not a luxury, but a norm.

5. Drainage: A Marvel of Ancient Sanitation

Mohenjo-Daro's most celebrated engineering achievement may be its citywide drainage system—a highly organized network of covered drains and soak pits that ran beneath or behind buildings, directing wastewater out of residential and public areas.

Drainage system features:

- Covered brick drains beneath streets and courtyards
- Regularly inspect holes and manholes for maintenance

- Slope engineering to ensure water flow via gravity

- Drains connected individual homes to the main sewer lines

- Terminal points included soak pits to filter waste before it returned to the earth

The existence of such a comprehensive public works system implies not only technical expertise, but also municipal organization—possibly an early form of city planning or civil service.

6. Stormwater Management and Flood Defense

Mohenjo-Daro's engineers also considered seasonal changes, particularly monsoon rains and flooding from the Indus River.

Protective features included:

- Elevated platforms for major structures like the Citadel and public buildings

- Use of drainage slopes and overflow routes for stormwater

- Perimeter walls and terracing to protect against erosion

- Periodic rebuilding of streets and buildings on raised debris layers, possibly in response to flooding or water damage

These adaptations indicate a dynamic and responsive approach to environmental challenges, ensuring that water remains a source of life, not destruction.

7. Engineering Tools and Materials

The success of Mohenjo-Daro's infrastructure relied on the consistent use of standardized materials and thoughtful design.

Key materials and techniques:

- Uniform baked bricks (proportioned at 1:2:4 dimensions)
- Use of bitumen (tar) for waterproofing in baths and drains
- Terracotta pipes and ring-formed clay toilets
- Wooden reinforcements in some structures, though few remain today

These technologies were not haphazard—they resulted from standardized construction practices, likely coordinated by guilds, city planners, or specialized engineers.

8. Cultural Significance of Cleanliness

The extraordinary focus on water and sanitation reflects more than technical achievement—it points to a cultural philosophy that valued cleanliness, order, and balance.

- Frequent depiction of water-related symbols on seals and figurines
- Ritual bathing suggested by public baths and bathing platforms
- Spatial separation of clean and unclean areas within homes
- Lack of litter or waste heaps in archaeological strata suggests strict civic discipline

Some scholars have linked this cultural ethos to later South Asian religious ideas, particularly in Hinduism, Buddhism, and Jainism, emphasizing purity, ritual washing, and environmental harmony.

Conclusion

Mohenjo-Daro's mastery of water management and sanitation was not an accident but a conscious, society-wide investment in health, ritual, and community welfare. In a world where most cities were plagued by filth and disease, Mohenjo-Daro flourished through planning, precision, and an ethic of cleanliness that remains stunningly modern.

The city's engineered wells, drainage networks, and bathing facilities reflect a blend of science, spirituality, and civic pride. More than any monument or text, this infrastructure speaks eloquently of the civilization's values, intellect, and foresight.

Though the people of Mohenjo-Daro left no written treatise on urban design, their city remains a living lesson in how water, when respected and regulated, can sustain life and legacy.

CHAPTER ELEVEN:
AGRICULTURE AND FOOD PRODUCTION

Introduction

At the heart of any enduring civilization lies the fundamental question: How did its people feed themselves? The answer for Mohenjo-Daro and the broader Indus Valley Civilization lies in a remarkably advanced and sustainable agriculture and food production system that supported dense urban populations, enabled long-distance trade, and fostered societal stability over centuries.

Unlike other early civilizations that often faced food crises due to over-farming or environmental instability, the Indus people appear to have developed a resilient agricultural base, supported by innovations in irrigation, crop diversity, and storage systems. This chapter delves into the methods, tools, and cultural implications of agriculture in Mohenjo-Daro, painting a picture of a civilization that not only cultivated the land but understood its rhythms.

1. The Indus and Its Fertile Plains

The Indus River and its tributaries formed the lifeblood of Mohenjo-Daro's agricultural success. The city was strategically located in a region where seasonal flooding deposited rich alluvial soil, making the land exceptionally fertile.

Environmental advantages:

- Annual floods replenished the soil without the need for artificial fertilizers
- The monsoon cycle provided a predictable rhythm for planting and harvesting
- A mix of arid and semi-arid zones allowed for varied farming techniques, from dry farming to flood-fed agriculture

This natural abundance enabled the people of Mohenjo-Daro to experiment with multiple crop cycles and cultivate a wide range of produce.

2. Primary Crops and Diet Staples

Archaeobotanical evidence—plant remains, seeds, and impressions found at various Indus sites—has revealed a diverse and adaptable agricultural regime.

Major cultivated crops included:

- Wheat and barley – core grains used for bread and porridge

- Millets and lentils – hardy crops suitable for arid zones

- Sesame and mustard – used for oil extraction and flavoring

- Cotton – one of the earliest known instances of cotton cultivation in the ancient world

- Rice – though less common in the western Indus, some evidence suggests its use in the eastern regions

This crop diversity provided nutritional stability and made the civilization resilient to climatic variations.

3. Irrigation and Water Management in Farming

Though the Indus River provided seasonal floodwaters, agriculture at Mohenjo-Daro required more than natural luck—intentional water management.

Possible irrigation techniques:

- Canals and water channels: Though few direct remains survive, layouts and leveled fields suggest that canal irrigation systems were in place

- Reservoirs and bunds: Earth embankments may have helped divert water or store it during drier months

- Wells: In smaller settlements and drier regions, wells were likely used for watering small fields or kitchen gardens

The existence of standardized water systems within cities reflects a larger cultural understanding of water as both a civic and agricultural asset.

4. Agricultural Tools and Techniques

While metal tools like ploughshares have rarely survived due to the region's soil conditions, terracotta models and wear patterns on land suggest a suite of farming instruments.

Tools and farming methods:

- Wooden ploughs: Pulled by oxen, used to turn the soil for seeding

- Sickles and blades: Likely used for harvesting; copper and bronze tools would have supplemented wooden ones

- Grinding stones and mortars: Found in abundance, used to process grains

- Storage jars and granaries: Indicate post-harvest processing and preservation strategies

The widespread presence of grain processing equipment within homes suggests that food preparation was a domestic, decentralized activity, likely carried out by women and family units.

5. Domesticated Animals and Animal Husbandry

Farming in Mohenjo-Daro was not limited to crops—it included animal husbandry, which played a central role in food production, transportation, and agricultural labor.

Common domesticated animals:

- Cattle and water buffalo – used for ploughing and milk
- Goats and sheep – sources of meat, wool, and hides
- Poultry – chickens and ducks provided meat and eggs
- Dogs – likely used for herding and protection
- Possibly elephants – suggested in some seals, perhaps domesticated for labor or ritual

The multi-use approach to livestock points to a society that maximizes every resource available for nutrition, textile production, and farming efficiency.

6. Food Processing, Storage, and Distribution

Feeding a city like Mohenjo-Daro required producing food and storing, preserving, and distributing it effectively.

Systems in place:

- Public granaries: Massive storage buildings likely used to collect and distribute grains during lean seasons

- Terracotta storage jars: Found in both public spaces and private homes

- Open courtyards: Used for drying grains, pulses, and produce

- Sealed storage pits: Possibly used to protect reserves from pests and moisture

These systems hint at some form of central oversight, perhaps involving administrators or grain managers who ensured equitable access and taxation in kind.

7. Diet and Culinary Practices

The variety of foods available in Mohenjo-Daro suggests a rich and balanced diet.

Likely components of the Indus diet:

- Grain-based breads and gruels made from wheat, barley, or millets

- Legume stews seasoned with mustard or turmeric

- Fruits like dates, jujubes, and melons

- Dairy products, including milk, yogurt, and possibly cheese

- Fish and meat, including beef, goat, fowl, and occasional wild game

Tools such as hearths, tandoor-style ovens, and cooking pots point to communal and domestic food preparation. The absence of elaborate dining ware suggests that meals were simple, shared, and utilitarian rather than ceremonial.

8. Agriculture and Social Organization

Agriculture wasn't just a food source but a social and economic engine.

- Land ownership and control of irrigation may have been tied to social hierarchy.

- Farmers and food producers likely held respected roles, though probably below merchants and administrators.

- Agricultural surplus enabled non-farming professions to flourish: artisans, traders, and scribes.

- Fertility rituals and seasonal festivals were likely connected to the agricultural calendar, linking spiritual life to food production.

The smooth integration of agriculture with other economic and cultural systems points to a balanced and well-managed society.

Conclusion

The agricultural achievements of Mohenjo-Daro were not only technical but deeply cultural. With its flood-fed fields, sophisticated irrigation, and seasonal diversity of crops, the Indus Valley Civilization developed one of the most sustainable and self-reliant food systems in the ancient world.

This mastery of land and water enabled the civilization to build great cities, support skilled labor, and establish trade routes stretching as far as Mesopotamia. More than mere survival, agriculture allowed for the flourishing of art, governance, and daily life.

In every grain of barley and every seed of cotton, the legacy of the Indus people lives on—not just as farmers, but as engineers of abundance, planners of prosperity, and stewards of the earth.

CHAPTER TWELVE:
TECHNOLOGY AND INNOVATION

Introduction

In the ancient world, the progress of a civilization was often measured by its ability to innovate—to craft tools, develop systems, and solve problems that allowed it to survive and thrive. In this regard, Mohenjo-Daro and the greater Indus Valley Civilization are beacons of ingenuity, remarkable for their technical achievements and subtle sophistication.

Though they left behind no deciphered texts, the material culture of the Indus people tells a powerful story. From their use of standardized weights and measures to their intricate craftsmanship, from metallurgy to proto-engineering, the citizens of Mohenjo-Daro lived in a technologically advanced society that understood the relationship between science, functionality, and beauty.

This chapter explores the technological innovations of Mohenjo-Daro—some visible in grand city structures, others hidden in the tools of daily life. Together, they reflect a people who were curious, creative, and deeply committed to order, utility, and refinement.

1. Urban Engineering: A Systematic Approach

Mohenjo-Daro's most prominent technological marvel lies in its urban infrastructure. The city's layout, with its grid-pattern streets, sewage systems, and well-planned buildings, reveals a high level of planning and foresight.

Hallmarks of Indus urban engineering:

- Orthogonal street grid: Streets intersect at right angles, suggesting planned development

- Standardized brick dimensions (1:2:4): A technological leap in modular construction

- Stormwater and sewage systems: Underground drains, soak pits, and access covers

- Zoning of residential, public, and industrial areas

Such precision was likely the result of trained architects or planners and may have required mathematical knowledge, including early geometry and spatial measurement concepts.

2. Weights, Measures, and Standardization

One of the Indus Valley Civilization's most astonishing achievements is its standardized weights and measures system, unmatched in consistency across hundreds of miles.

Features of the measurement system:

- Cubic weights of chert stone are often marked in binary progressions (1, 2, 4, 8, etc.)

- Uniformity of measuring tools and devices, suggesting regulation or a central authority

- Evidence of rulers or measuring rods made of ivory, marked with precise divisions

- The same weight system was used in trade, construction, and crafts

This system facilitated internal commerce and long-distance trade, indicating a shared understanding of value and quantity across regions—a rare accomplishment for the ancient world.

3. Metallurgy and Material Mastery

The people of Mohenjo-Daro were among the first to precisely manipulate metals, particularly copper, bronze, lead, and even traces of iron. Their metallurgy served both utilitarian and decorative purposes.

Metalworking achievements:

- Copper and bronze tools: Axes, knives, chisels, and fishhooks

- Jewelry made from gold, silver, copper, and semi-precious stones

- Casting techniques: The lost-wax method is evident in small sculptures like the famous "Dancing Girl."

- Evidence of furnaces and smelting workshops in some urban zones

Their command of metal reflected craftsmanship and knowledge of ore extraction, alloying, and thermal manipulation.

4. Pottery and Kiln Technology

The pottery of Mohenjo-Daro is both functional and artistically expressive, produced using advanced kiln techniques and uniform methods.

Innovations in ceramic production:

- Use of wheel-thrown pottery, indicating mechanical assistance
- Firing in multi-chamber kilns capable of controlling heat levels
- Decorative elements such as slips, glazes, and motifs—from animal figures to geometric bands
- A variety of vessels for cooking, storage, rituals, and transport

The standardization in form and size again points to industrial-scale production, perhaps governed by guilds or overseen by city officials.

5. Craftsmanship and Technological Artistry

The artifacts of Mohenjo-Daro showcase a blend of technology and aesthetics, evident in beadwork, figurines, metalware, and seal carving.

Noteworthy examples:

- Beads of carnelian, agate, and lapis lazuli, drilled with remarkable precision using bow drills and abrasive slurry
- Terracotta figurines of animals, humans, and mythic creatures—often used for ritual or symbolic purposes

- Steatite seals engraved with animals and symbols, many with perforations suggesting use as amulets or trade tags

- Tools for textile production, including spindles and weights, hint at a vibrant clothing industry supported by technology.

These crafts required artistic talent and specialized knowledge of physics, materials, and tooling techniques.

6. Transportation and Mechanics

Trade and communication across the vast Indus Valley required mobility, and the people of Mohenjo-Daro developed vehicles and transport systems suited to their geography.

Transportation technologies:

- Bullock carts: Two-wheeled carts pulled by oxen, some evidenced by miniature terracotta models

- Boat use: Likely for trade along the Indus River and its tributaries—several dock-like structures and depictions on seals suggest river navigation.

- Standardized cart axle widths: Wheel tracks in streets imply uniformity in vehicle design

Such systems enhanced trade and connected urban centers, fostering economic integration and technological consistency across regions.

7. Water Technology and Hydraulic Innovation

As discussed in Chapter Ten, Mohenjo-Daro's water systems are one of the most sophisticated examples of ancient hydraulic engineering.

Water-related innovations:

- Private and public wells: Over 700 identified
- Covered drains and underground sewer lines
- Bathing platforms and latrines within homes
- Reservoirs or cisterns are used for water storage or flood control

This degree of water management was likely supported by trial-and-error engineering, inherited knowledge, and civic regulation, making Mohenjo-Daro a leader in public health and infrastructure.

8. Proto-Writing and Symbolic Systems

While the Indus script remains undeciphered (as explored in Chapter Eight), its existence suggests an intellectual culture rooted in recording and symbolic thinking.

Technological aspects of proto-writing:

- Symbols carved onto standardized steatite seals, often using microlithic tools
- Repetition of glyphs in structured patterns suggests a codified language or accounting system

- Some seals appear to be administrative tokens, possibly used for tracking goods, ownership, or identities.

Even without decipherment, the script reflects a society needing recordkeeping, authentication, and information transmission.

9. Innovation Without Monumentalism

Unlike contemporary civilizations that built colossal monuments, pyramids, or ziggurats, Mohenjo-Daro's innovations were primarily practical, civic, and human-centered.

Their focus lay not in glorifying rulers but in improving daily life:

- Better housing
- Cleaner water
- Reliable infrastructure

- Scalable tools and systems

This speaks to a different philosophical orientation toward innovation, prioritizing collective well-being over spectacle.

Conclusion

Technology at Mohenjo-Daro was neither ornamental nor accidental—it was deliberate, systematized, and integrative, forming the very backbone of urban life. The people of the Indus Valley excelled not through monumental display, but through quiet mastery of materials, measurements, mechanics, and methods.

Their legacy is not measured in towering ruins, but in the elegance of a brick, the consistency of a weight, the precision of a seal. They remind us that civilization is not built on awe alone, but on the countless innovations that make life livable, sustainable, and meaningful.

Mohenjo-Daro's story is not just one of the past—it's a blueprint for how societies can thrive through ingenuity, adaptability, and civic-minded technology.

CHAPTER THIRTEEN: RELATIONS WITH CONTEMPORARY CIVILIZATIONS

Introduction

The greatness of a civilization is not measured solely by what it builds within, but also by how it engages with the world beyond. Though often perceived as isolated, the Indus Valley Civilization—of which Mohenjo-Daro was a central hub—was anything but insular. Emerging around 2600 BCE, it existed alongside other major ancient civilizations like Mesopotamia, Egypt, and later, early Chinese cultures. Despite vast distances, the Indus people established trade networks, cultural exchanges, and technological dialogues that testify to their outward-looking, connected world.

This chapter explores how Mohenjo-Daro and the broader Indus society interacted with contemporary civilizations, uncovering threads of commerce, diplomacy, and cultural influence that stitched together the ancient world.

1. A Geostrategic Advantage

Mohenjo-Daro's location in the lower Indus valley gave it easy access to multiple geographic zones:

- The Arabian Sea for maritime trade

- The Persian Plateau to the west

- The Himalayas and the Hindu Kush to the north

- The Ganges Valley to the east

This strategic position allowed Mohenjo-Daro to act as a cultural crossroads and economic gateway between South Asia and the wider world. The city's dock-like structures and uniform trade goods suggest regular contact with external peoples, both near and far.

2. Trade with Mesopotamia: The Meluhha Connection

Among the most documented relationships is the one between the Indus Civilization and Mesopotamia, particularly the Sumerians and Akkadians.

Archaeological and textual evidence:

- Mesopotamian cuneiform texts refer to a land called "Meluhha", widely believed to be the Indus region.

- Goods such as carnelian beads, ivory, lapis lazuli, and cotton textiles from the Indus were found in Mesopotamian cities like Ur and Lagash.

- Mesopotamian seals and tablets mention Meluhhan merchants and interpreters, implying the presence of Indus traders in foreign lands.

- The dockyard at Lothal, another Indus site, suggests organized maritime commerce—possibly with ships bound for the Persian Gulf and Mesopotamia.

This contact was commercial and cultural, seen in shared motifs like the unicorn symbol and the use of weights and measures resembling Indus standards.

3. Connections with Central Asia and Iran

To the northwest of Mohenjo-Daro lay the Iranian plateau and Central Asia, regions with which the Indus people shared long-standing ties.

Shared material culture:

- Pottery styles and metallurgical techniques in Shahr-e Sukhteh (Burnt City, in present-day Iran) mirror those in the Indus Valley.

- Indus-style seals have been uncovered at sites such as Susa and Tepe Yahya, indicating trade and perhaps diplomatic gift exchange.

- The route through Baluchistan and the Bolan Pass was a corridor for migration, goods, and ideas.

These interactions helped fuel technological diffusion, particularly in metallurgy, and may have facilitated the spread of writing systems or ideograms.

4. Maritime Routes: The Arabian Peninsula and East Africa

Mohenjo-Daro's maritime capabilities likely enabled trade beyond the immediate region.

Indicators of far-reaching sea trade:

- Discoveries of Indus artifacts in Oman and Bahrain, including etched carnelian beads and seals.

- Bitumen from Mesopotamia found in Indus sites may have been used to waterproof ships.

- Shells from the Arabian Gulf and Red Sea regions appear in Indus ornaments.

- Some scholars speculate that indirect trade will reach East Africa, though evidence remains limited.

Such journeys would have required both navigational skills and logistical organization, shipbuilding technology, and knowledge of seasonal monsoon winds.

5. Influence on and from Neighboring Civilizations

The Indus Valley Civilization was both an exporter and importer of ideas.

Possible areas of influence:

- Urban planning principles, such as grid layouts and drainage, may have inspired elements in early West Asian cities.

- Symbolism and motifs found in Indus seals have analogues in later Mesopotamian religious imagery.

- Craft techniques like bead drilling and metallurgy were possibly shared or adapted across regions.

    Conversely, influences likely entered Mohenjo-Daro as well:

- Decorative styles, including geometric patterns on pottery, show similarities to Central Asian and Elamite traditions.

- The concept of seals for trade authentication may have been adapted from Mesopotamian models, or vice versa.

This reciprocal exchange underscores the fluidity of cultural borders in the Bronze Age.

6. Lack of Militarism and Diplomacy

Unlike Mesopotamia or Egypt, the Indus Valley Civilization left no evidence of standing armies, kings, or imperial conquests. Yet it still managed to maintain strong external relations.

Possible explanations:

- Trade-based diplomacy may have substituted for formal military alliances.

- Standardized seals and weights could have served as universal "passports" for merchants.

- Mutual dependence on trade commodities such as copper, tin, and lapis lazuli may have encouraged peace.

This economic diplomacy—based on commerce rather than conquest—may explain the long-lasting, stable exchanges with neighbors.

7. Comparison with Egypt and China

Though direct contact with Egypt and early Chinese civilizations is unlikely, comparing them offers perspective on the uniqueness of the Indus Civilization's relational model.

Feature	Egypt	Indus Valley	China (Early Shang)
Writing	Hieroglyphs	Undeciphered script	Oracle bone script
Government	Theocratic monarchy	Possibly decentralized	Divine kingship
Foreign Policy	Expansionist, imperial	Trade-based, non-militaristic	Isolationist with periodic trade
Architecture	Monumental (pyramids)	Civic (baths, drains)	Ancestral temples, palaces

Mohenjo-Daro's focus on internal refinement and peaceful exchange starkly contrasts with the militaristic ambitions of its contemporaries.

8. Enduring Legacy of Global Engagement

Though Mohenjo-Daro and its sister cities vanished mysteriously around 1900 BCE, their non-violent, economically driven, and technologically informed global engagement model remains relevant.

- The cosmopolitanism of the Indus people is seen in their goods, art, and infrastructure.

- Their legacy influenced South Asian cultures later, particularly in terms of trade traditions and urban layout.

- Elements of their technological ingenuity continued through the Bronze Age into the Iron Age civilizations of the subcontinent.

In many ways, the Indus Valley Civilization anticipated a globalized mindset, recognizing the value of connectivity long before modern globalization emerged.

Conclusion

Mohenjo-Daro was not an isolated island of progress—it was a vital node in an ancient web of civilizations, linking South Asia to the broader Bronze Age world. Through trade, technology, and cultural dialogue, its people forged relationships that spanned deserts, mountains, and oceans.

Their world was vast and interconnected, their vision outward-facing and inclusive. They remind us that even in antiquity, civilizations were not sealed containers, but living systems shaped as much by their neighbors as by their own hands.

The story of Mohenjo-Daro's relations with its contemporaries is one of peaceful exchange, sophisticated coordination, and enduring influence—a testament to how global understanding can flourish without war, empire, or dominance.

CHAPTER FOURTEEN: THEORIES OF DECLINE AND ABANDONMENT

Introduction

Few stories in ancient history are as mysterious as the fall of Mohenjo-Daro and the broader Indus Valley Civilization. Once thriving with advanced urban infrastructure, robust trade, and sophisticated technology, these cities experienced a sudden and enigmatic decline around 1900 BCE. Streets emptied. Craft workshops fell silent. Trade routes vanished. The Great Bath, once a symbol of civic pride, was left to gather dust and debris.

Why did one of the world's most advanced Bronze Age civilizations collapse? The truth remains elusive, locked behind undeciphered scripts and silent ruins. Yet scholars have proposed several compelling theories, ranging from environmental shifts and natural disasters to socio-political changes and external invasions. None are definitive, but they offer a mosaic of possibilities.

This chapter examines the leading theories behind the decline and abandonment of Mohenjo-Daro, highlighting the complexity of societal collapse and the lessons it holds for civilizations, ancient and modern alike.

1. Environmental Changes and Climate Shifts

Among the most widely supported explanations for the decline of the Indus was a dramatic change in climate and river systems, particularly the drying up or shifting of rivers that sustained civilization.

Key environmental factors:

- Desiccation of the Ghaggar-Hakra (Saraswati?) River: Once believed to be a major artery of civilization, its disappearance would have crippled agriculture and inland trade.

- Weakened monsoon patterns: Climate reconstructions show a gradual weakening of the Indian summer monsoon around 2000–1900 BCE, leading to lower rainfall.

- Decline in groundwater tables: Urban wells in Mohenjo-Daro may have dried up, making daily life unsustainable.

- Drought conditions: Evidence from lake sediments and fossilized pollen points to several centuries of regional drought.

Impacts on Mohenjo-Daro:

- Shrinking agricultural output
- Pressure on food storage and water systems
- Rural-to-urban migration is reversing, leading to urban depopulation

This ecological fragility highlights the dependence of advanced societies on stable environments and how even subtle shifts can lead to systemic unraveling.

2. Tectonic Activity and Flooding

Mohenjo-Daro's location on the floodplains of the Indus River rendered it vulnerable to earthquakes and floods, two natural forces that may have accelerated its demise.

Geological and hydrological evidence:

- The city shows layers of silt that suggest repeated inundations—possibly massive floods or waterlogging from river course shifts.

- Changes in the Indus River's path could have undermined the city's drainage and sanitation systems.

- Earthquake-prone zones in the region point to possible tectonic disturbances that disrupted river flows and damaged infrastructure.

Unlike cities adapted to seasonal flooding (like those in Egypt), Mohenjo-Daro lacked large-scale levees or dams, making it vulnerable to sudden environmental shocks.

3. Economic Decline and Trade Disruption

Trade was a lifeline for Mohenjo-Daro. When that line frayed, the consequences were felt across the civilization.

Possible trade-related causes:

- The collapse of external trading partners, such as Mesopotamia, saw disruptions around 2000 BCE due to Elamite invasions and internal conflicts.

- Decline in maritime trade due to shifting river mouths or coastline changes.

- Internal disintegration of commercial systems, including standardized weights and seals.

As trade waned, so did the urban centers that depended on it. Mohenjo-Daro may have become economically unsustainable, forcing inhabitants to return to rural lifestyles.

4. Sociopolitical Fragmentation

Unlike Mesopotamia or Egypt, the Indus Civilization left no evidence of centralized kingship or standing armies. While this may have fostered peace in stable times, it also meant that there may have been no unified leadership to coordinate responses during crises.

Signs of social instability:

- Urban planning becomes less standardized in later phases.
- Public works and sanitation systems fall into disrepair.
- Artifacts show a decline in craftsmanship and production scale.
- Evidence of squatter-style housing over older structures suggests growing poverty and desperation.

This points to a fragmented society, unable to maintain the complexity that once defined it.

5. Aryan Invasion or Migration Theory (Contested)

Once a dominant theory, the idea that Indo-Aryan-speaking migrants or invaders contributed to the collapse has since lost much academic support, but it remains part of historical discourse.

Elements of the theory:

- Based on later Vedic texts describing the destruction of "fortified cities" by Aryan tribes.

- Some early excavators pointed to skeletal remains at Mohenjo-Daro as evidence of a massacre.

- The decline of urban centers coincides roughly with the arrival of Indo-European linguistic groups into northwest India.

Scholarly critique:

- There is no archaeological evidence of warfare, large-scale destruction, or mass graves linked to the invasion.

- Skeletal injuries could be from natural causes or isolated violence, not conquest.

- Cultural continuity in pottery, tools, and village life suggests evolution, not replacement.

Today, the Aryan Invasion Theory has mainly been reframed as gradual migration and cultural integration, not a violent collapse.

6. Disease and Epidemic Hypothesis

Another speculative but intriguing theory posits that disease—possibly waterborne or zoonotic—led to sudden population decline.

Supporting observations:

- Dense urban living and poor sanitation during flood events could have created breeding grounds for cholera or typhoid.

- A few sites show abrupt abandonment, with skeletons left unburied in situ, possibly suggesting a fast-spreading epidemic.

- Rodent- or insect-borne diseases may have traveled via trade routes, affecting multiple cities.

-

While hard to prove without genetic or epidemiological data, this theory reminds us that biological threats have long shaped human history.

7. Multicausal and Gradual Decline

The most widely accepted view today is that no single cause explains the fall of Mohenjo-Daro. Instead, scholars argue for a multicausal, gradual decline over several generations.

Contributing factors, in combination:

- Environmental degradation reduced agricultural viability.

- Trade decline undermined urban economies.

- Sociopolitical weakness hindered the response to crises.

- Natural disasters periodically devastated infrastructure.

- Ruralization replaced urbanism as people dispersed into smaller settlements.

Rather than a sudden cataclysm, the civilization appears to have withered slowly, its cities abandoned over decades, its innovations absorbed into emerging cultural identities.

8. Life After Mohenjo-Daro

The story did not end with abandonment. Descendants of the Indus people likely migrated eastward, influencing later cultures in the Gangetic plains and beyond.

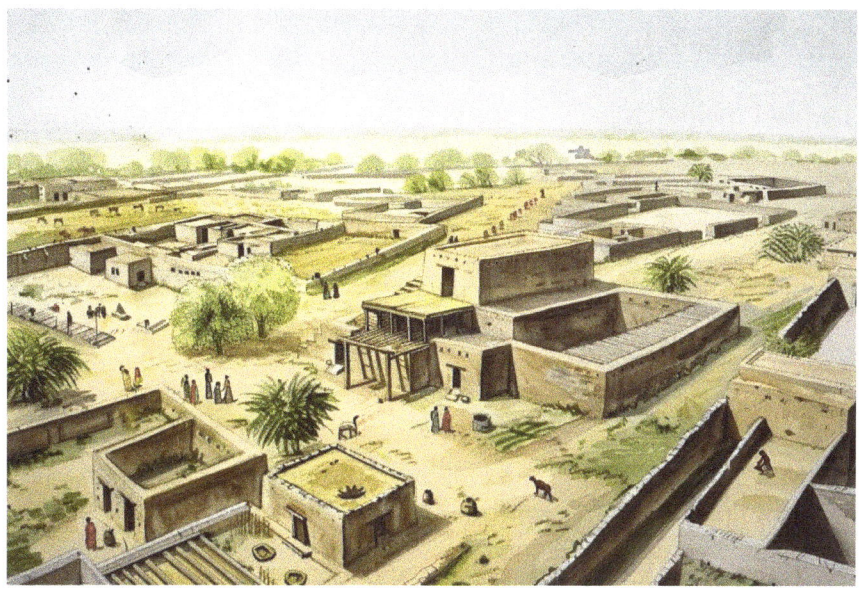

Cultural continuities:

- Techniques in pottery, agriculture, and village layout persist into the Painted Grey Ware and Vedic periods.

- Indus-like symbols and motifs appear sporadically in later South Asian art and craft.

- Oral traditions and early Hindu cosmology may contain echoes of Indus myth and ritual.

Thus, while Mohenjo-Daro the city fell, Mohenjo-Daro the civilization lived on, transformed but unforgotten.

Conclusion

The fall of Mohenjo-Daro is not a tale of defeat, but a profound lesson in the fragility of complex societies. Its decline may have been slow, silent, and dispersed—but in that silence lies wisdom. It shows how even the most advanced systems can falter when climate shifts, infrastructure ages, trade falters, and leadership is absent.

Yet the ruins also whisper of resilience. The people adapted, moved, and redefined their identity in new regions. What endures is not only mystery, but also legacy—the bricks, drains, and seals that continue to speak, centuries later.

In the next and final chapter, we will explore that legacy—how the memory of Mohenjo-Daro has shaped South Asia's cultural imagination, inspired scholars, and challenged us to rethink what it means for a civilization to rise, fall, and endure.

CHAPTER FIFTEEN: MODERN REDISCOVERY AND ARCHAEOLOGICAL LEGACY

Introduction

For over three millennia, the city of Mohenjo-Daro lay buried beneath layers of earth and time—its people forgotten, its streets silent, its language unread. Unlike ancient Egypt or Mesopotamia, whose civilizations were known through classical texts, the Indus Valley Civilization remained hidden from historical memory, absent from mythologies and chronicles alike. Its rediscovery in the 20th century stunned the world, forcing scholars to rewrite the very foundations of ancient history.

Mohenjo-Daro was not just an archaeological site—it was a revelation. Its rediscovery uncovered a civilization rivaling its better-known contemporaries in complexity, sophistication, and scale. This chapter traces the journey of that rediscovery—from the first accidental sightings to the monumental excavations, and the enduring legacy that continues to shape archaeology, heritage, and national identity today.

1. Early Clues and Forgotten Ruins

Before its scientific excavation, the ruins of Mohenjo-Daro were little more than anonymous mounds. Locals referred to them as "Mound of the Dead", unaware of the significance buried below.

Early observations:

- In the 19th century, British engineers and railway workers encountered fired bricks and pottery while laying tracks in the Indus region.

- Charles Masson, a British deserter turned antiquarian, noted unusual ruins in the 1830s but mistook them for Buddhist relics.

- The authentic antiquity of the site was not suspected due to the lack of inscriptions in known scripts or monumental structures like pyramids or ziggurats.

It would take decades to realize that these scattered remnants belonged to one of the oldest urban civilizations.

2. The Breakthrough: Excavations Begin

The genuine rediscovery of Mohenjo-Daro came in the 1920s, under the guidance of the Archaeological Survey of India (ASI).

Key figures:

- Sir John Marshall, Director-General of the ASI, was pivotal in promoting systematic excavation.

- Rakhaldas Banerji, an Indian archaeologist, identified brickwork and seals that hinted at antiquity.

- Excavations began in 1924, revealing a well-planned city with streets, drains, and public buildings—unlike anything seen in South Asia.

This was not a provincial outpost or religious shrine. It was a fully developed city that belonged to a contemporary civilization, along with ancient Egypt and Mesopotamia.

3. A Civilization Emerges

Similar finds at Harappa, Lothal, Kalibangan, and Dholavira soon followed the discovery of Mohenjo-Daro. Together, these sites redefined the boundaries of ancient civilization.

What the findings revealed:

- A vast urban culture spanning over a million square kilometers.

- Standardized weights, measures, and architectural layouts across multiple cities.

- Seals with unknown script, fired bricks, granaries, and the now-famous Great Bath.

- A civilization with no known rulers or military monuments, yet showing remarkable administrative control.

The discovery challenged Eurocentric historical narratives and elevated the Indian subcontinent as a cradle of early complex society.

4. Preservation Challenges and UNESCO Recognition

As excavations deepened, so did concerns over preserving this delicate site.

Threats to the site:

- Exposure to the elements led to salt crystallization, weakening bricks.

- Poor water drainage and a high water table posed erosion risks.

- Earlier excavation techniques lacked modern conservation foresight, leading to structural damage in some areas.

In 1980, Mohenjo-Daro was declared a UNESCO World Heritage Site, drawing global attention to its plight. Conservation efforts were ramped up, with emphasis on:

- Halting further large-scale excavation
- Strengthening exposed structures
- Monitoring environmental conditions

Preserving Mohenjo-Daro is not just about saving a site—it's about protecting the legacy of a lost civilization for future generations.

5. Mohenjo-Daro in National and Cultural Identity

For Pakistan, where Mohenjo-Daro is located, the site has become a powerful symbol of national pride and historical identity.

Cultural and educational impact:

- The site is featured in school textbooks, currency notes, and national museums.

- Annual conferences and exhibitions celebrate the city's legacy.

- The Mohenjo-Daro Cultural Festival, though controversial for preservationists, underscores its role in the public imagination.

For India, the broader Indus Civilization also forms a critical chapter in historical education, academic research, and cultural pride. It represents a shared heritage that predates modern borders, reminding all South Asians of a common, ancient past.

6. Advances in Archaeological Techniques

Modern technologies have revolutionized how archaeologists study Mohenjo-Daro without disturbing its fragile layers.

Non-invasive methods include:

- Ground-penetrating radar (GPR) to map buried structures

- Remote sensing and satellite imagery to analyze city layout

- Isotope analysis of human remains to study diet and migration

- 3D reconstructions and virtual tours to digitally preserve the site

These techniques allow scholars to ask new questions without risking damage, bringing the ancient city to life for new generations.

7. The Indus Script: A Lingering Enigma

Despite extensive excavation, one mystery remains stubbornly unsolved: the Indus script.

- Over 4,000 inscriptions have been found, mostly short, stamped on seals and tablets.

- The script remains undeciphered, with no Rosetta Stone equivalent.

- Attempts to decode it using linguistic, statistical, and AI-driven methods continue, but no consensus exists.

Until the script is deciphered, many aspects of Indus society—religion, politics, and daily affairs—remain shadows on the wall.

8. Global Legacy and Continuing Relevance

The rediscovery of Mohenjo-Daro has influenced not only historians but also architects, planners, artists, and environmentalists.

Lasting contributions:

- Urban planners study their drainage systems as early models of sustainable design.

- Artists and writers draw inspiration from its symbols, script, and myths.

- Scholars explore how non-hierarchical societies can still build complex systems.

Mohenjo-Daro offers timeless lessons in planning, resource use, and civic organization in an age of climate change, overpopulation, and urban stress.

Conclusion

The modern rediscovery of Mohenjo-Daro was more than an archaeological milestone—it was a civilizational awakening. In its buried streets and broken seals, the ancient city told a story no one expected: that a complex, peaceful, technologically advanced society once thrived in the heart of South Asia, long before the classical empires of history.

Today, Mohenjo-Daro stands at a crossroads—a treasure of the past and a responsibility of the present. Preserving history is not just about honoring history but learning from it. As we move into the future, the city continues to challenge, inspire, and remind us that greatness lies not just in war monuments, but in systems of peace, order, and human ingenuity.

CHAPTER SIXTEEN: PRESERVATION AND THREATS TODAY

Introduction

Mohenjo-Daro, once a beacon of ancient urban brilliance, now stands at the mercy of time, nature, and human neglect. As one of the most iconic archaeological sites of the ancient world, its preservation is of national importance for Pakistan and is of global heritage significance. Yet, despite being a UNESCO World Heritage Site since 1980, Mohenjo-Daro faces mounting threats that endanger its survival. This chapter examines the contemporary state of preservation, outlines the challenges that threaten the site, and explores the ongoing and needed efforts to secure its legacy for future generations.

1. The Fragile State of the Site

Mohenjo-Daro was not built to last 5,000 years. Unlike Egyptian pyramids or stone-carved temples, its architecture relies heavily on sun-dried and fired bricks, vulnerable to erosion and environmental damage.

Factors contributing to fragility:

- Exposure to moisture from seasonal rains and rising groundwater causes brick decay.

- Salinity and salt crystallization deteriorate the structures from within.

- High humidity and temperature fluctuations lead to thermal stress on the ancient walls.

- Lack of protective roofing or modern conservation techniques during early excavations has worsened the deterioration.

The city that once mastered water management is now slowly being undone by the elements it once controlled.

2. Climate Change and Environmental Stress

The broader issue of climate change has directly impacted Mohenjo-Daro's preservation.

Environmental threats:

- Heavier monsoon rains in recent years have led to increased flooding and saturation of the site.

- Increased salinity in the water table, partly due to agricultural irrigation in the surrounding areas, accelerates brick corrosion.

- Soil erosion and river movement threaten the mound's structural stability.

Without urgent environmental monitoring and drainage solutions, future climate volatility could spell disaster for the site.

3. Human Impact and Mismanagement

Beyond natural forces, human negligence and administrative missteps have also placed Mohenjo-Daro at risk.

Problematic human activities:

- Unregulated tourism leads to wear and tear, especially on footpaths and staircases not designed for modern foot traffic.

- Cultural events held at the site—such as concerts or political gatherings—have caused vibrations and damage to fragile remains.

- Encroachment and development in nearby areas threaten the integrity of the archaeological zone.

- There have been theft and illegal artifact trade, particularly in the early 20th century.

Moreover, fragmented management—often divided between federal, provincial, and local bodies—has resulted in conflicting policies and underfunded conservation programs.

4. International Support and Conservation Initiatives

Despite the challenges, national and international bodies have taken steps to protect Mohenjo-Daro.

Major efforts include:

- UNESCO's 20-Year Master Plan (initiated in the 1980s) was to stabilize the ruins and prevent further decay.

- The establishment of the Mohenjo-Daro Conservation Cell was tasked with implementing emergency measures and maintenance protocols.

- Collaboration with international archaeologists and heritage engineers to develop sustainable conservation practices.

- Public education campaigns in Pakistan are being conducted to raise awareness of the site's significance.

Organizations like the World Monuments Fund and the German Archaeological Institute have also contributed technical expertise and funds.

5. The Need for Sustainable Preservation

Mohenjo-Daro's preservation cannot be achieved by restoration alone—it requires a sustainable, long-term approach that addresses root causes.

Recommendations for sustainable conservation:

- Introduce protective shelter structures over key parts of the site to reduce direct exposure to rain and sun.

- Implement water management systems to regulate groundwater levels and prevent salt accumulation.

- Develop strict visitor guidelines, including designated walkways, capacity limits, and virtual tourism alternatives.

- Promote community involvement by training locals in

conservation and fostering pride in cultural heritage.

- Encourage academic partnerships with global institutions for continued research and innovation in conservation science.

Preservation must be adaptive, proactive, and grounded in scientific rigor and cultural sensitivity.

6. The Role of Digital Technology

Digital tools now offer powerful ways to preserve and share Mohenjo-Daro's legacy without endangering the site.

Technological innovations include:

- 3D scanning and modeling of structures to record precise architectural details before further decay occurs.

- Virtual reality (VR) experiences provide immersive access to the site, reducing physical tourism pressure.

- GIS mapping and drone photography to monitor erosion and structural changes over time.

- Digital archiving of inscriptions, seals, and artifacts for global scholarly access.

These technologies can help Mohenjo-Daro remain accessible, studied, and celebrated, without being physically overwhelmed.

7. A Shared Global Responsibility

Though located in Pakistan, Mohenjo-Daro is not the legacy of one nation alone—it belongs to the world.

Global significance:

- It is one of only a handful of Bronze Age cities with advanced civic planning that predates classical antiquity.

- Its lessons in urban sustainability, non-violent social organization, and technological innovation remain relevant today.

- Preserving it means honoring humanity's collective past, ensuring that future generations can learn from its wisdom and wonder.

Mohenjo-Daro is not just an archaeological site. It is a mirror of civilization—of what we are capable of, and what we must protect.

Conclusion: The Future of Mohenjo-Daro

The ancient city that once mastered water, trade, and urban harmony now stands vulnerable to waterlogging, neglect, and climate disruption. But Mohenjo-Daro's story does not have to end in ruin. Through informed policy, technological support, international collaboration, and public engagement, we can ensure that this jewel of the ancient world continues to teach, inspire, and endure.

The survival of Mohenjo-Daro is not simply about saving bricks and ruins. It is about preserving one of humanity's earliest experiments in civilization—its successes, mysteries, and wisdom. It calls on all of us—scholars, citizens, policymakers, and dreamers—to become its stewards.

Because if Mohenjo-Daro disappears, we don't just lose a city—we lose a part of ourselves.

CHAPTER SEVENTEEN: MOHENJO-DARO IN POPULAR CULTURE AND EDUCATION

Introduction

Though silent for over 4,000 years, Mohenjo-Daro continues to echo in the modern world—not only through excavation sites and academic discourse but also in classrooms, museums, literature, film, and popular imagination. As one of the most iconic relics of the ancient Indus Valley Civilization, it has transformed from an archaeological marvel into a cultural symbol—a bridge between antiquity and the present.

This chapter explores how Mohenjo-Daro has permeated popular culture, shaped national consciousness, inspired artistic representations, and influenced South Asia's educational systems.

1. Mohenjo-Daro in National Identity and Symbolism

Mohenjo-Daro serves as a cultural and historical touchstone for both Pakistan and India.

In Pakistan:

- The site is featured on currency notes, stamps, and tourism campaigns.

- It symbolizes the deep roots of civilization on Pakistani soil, predating Islamic, Vedic, and colonial periods.

- Government institutions, museums, and cultural festivals invoke Mohenjo-Daro as a proud emblem of heritage.

In India:

- While the physical site lies in present-day Pakistan, the civilization is shared, predating modern borders.

- The Indus Valley Civilization is presented in school curricula as an integral part of Indian antiquity.

- Cultural references to Harappa and Mohenjo-Daro are standard in Indian popular culture, literature, and historical fiction.

Thus, Mohenjo-Daro stands as a symbol of shared ancestry, cutting across the political divisions of the subcontinent.

2. Representations in Film and Media

Mohenjo-Daro has inspired numerous creative interpretations, from documentaries to fictionalized films. These works range in accuracy and intent, from educational to entertainment-driven.

Notable examples:

- Documentaries by the BBC, National Geographic, and Pakistani producers have examined the site's history, mystery, and architecture.

- The 2016 Bollywood film *Mohenjo-Daro*, directed by Ashutosh Gowariker and starring Hrithik Roshan, attempted a fictionalized narrative set in the ancient city.

While the film was criticized for historical inaccuracies and anachronisms, it also reignited public interest in the civilization.

- Television shows, YouTube documentaries, and podcast episodes across multiple languages frequently explore Mohenjo-Daro as a topic of mystery and wonder.

These media portrayals, whether factual or fictional, play a key role in popularizing the legacy of the Indus Valley Civilization for global audiences.

3. Mohenjo-Daro in Literature and the Arts

Writers, poets, and artists have long drawn upon the mythology, mystery, and aesthetic of Mohenjo-Daro.

Literary influence:

- Historical novels and children's books have reimagined life in the ancient city, often with fictional characters navigating a world of markets, crafts, and early governance.

- Urdu, Hindi, Sindhi, and English poets have written elegies to the "dead city," symbolizing lost grandeur or humanity's forgotten past.

- The motif of undeciphered language—the Indus script—has been used as a metaphor for forgotten love, silence, or buried truths.

Artistic depictions:

- Visual artists have recreated scenes of daily life, city layouts, and imagined rituals based on archaeological interpretations.

- Seals, motifs, and pottery designs are frequently used in contemporary jewelry, textiles, and ceramics, bridging the past with modern craft traditions.

Mohenjo-Daro, thus, lives not just in stones but in storytelling, symbolism, and style.

4. The Role of Mohenjo-Daro in Education

Education has played a vital role in embedding Mohenjo-Daro into public consciousness, especially in South Asia.

In Pakistani curricula:

- Taught as part of Social Studies and History at the primary and secondary school levels.
- Emphasis on the Indus people's technological, urban, and cultural achievements.
- Often tied to lessons on national pride and heritage preservation.

In Indian curricula:

- Featured prominently in NCERT history textbooks, with visual illustrations and comparative analysis with other ancient civilizations.
- Students often learn about the Great Bath, granaries, seals, and city planning with classroom discussions and model-building projects.

In global academia:

- Mohenjo-Daro is a standard topic in introductory archaeology, ancient history, and South Asian university studies programs.
- Scholars use it to teach concepts of urbanism, state formation, early trade, and undeciphered scripts.

Formal and informal educational outreach continues to be a powerful cultural preservation and awareness tool.

5. Museums and Public Exhibits

Museums play a pivotal role in making the story of Mohenjo-Daro tangible for a global audience.

Major institutions with Indus Valley exhibits:

- The National Museum of Pakistan (Karachi) houses artifacts like pottery, jewelry, tools, and the iconic *Priest-King* statue.

- Lahore Museum and Sindh Museum (Hyderabad) also contain significant collections from the site.

- India's National Museum (New Delhi) features Indus artifacts like the *Dancing Girl*, a bronze statuette from Mohenjo-Daro.

- The British Museum and the Smithsonian Institution have displayed traveling exhibitions featuring Indus Valley items.

Interactive exhibits, 3D reconstructions, and VR experiences are increasingly used to bring the ancient city to life for younger audiences and international visitors.

6. Challenges in Representation and Misinterpretation

Despite widespread interest, Mohenjo-Daro is often misrepresented or oversimplified in popular culture.

Common challenges:

- Fictionalized portrayals often conflate it with mythological or Vedic narratives without historical evidence.

- Egypt and Mesopotamia sometimes overshadow the civilization in global discussions of early history.

- Limited understanding of the Indus script means much of the culture is open to speculation, which can lead to pseudohistorical claims or sensationalism.

Addressing these requires responsible storytelling, accurate educational content, and critical historical engagement.

7. A Living Legacy

Mohenjo-Daro is not just a subject of study—it is a living legacy.

- Cultural festivals and school exhibitions continue to celebrate their influence.

- Young artists, filmmakers, and designers use it as a creative source.

- Communities near the site—especially in Sindh—see it as part of their ancestral and cultural identity.

Mohenjo-Daro may be ancient, but it remains profoundly relevant as a source of inspiration, pride, and a cautionary tale.

Conclusion: The Eternal City in Modern Minds

Mohenjo-Daro has journeyed far from its original purpose as a Bronze Age city. Today, it lives on as a cultural icon, a symbol of human ingenuity, and a quiet challenge to the modern world: remembering, learning, and preserving. Whether in classrooms or cinema, art or digital media, its spirit endures—bridging the ancient with the contemporary.

As long as we continue to tell its story—thoughtfully, creatively, and truthfully—Mohenjo-Daro will never truly be lost.

CHAPTER EIGHTEEN: FUTURE RESEARCH AND UNANSWERED QUESTIONS

Introduction

Despite nearly a century of excavation and study, Mohenjo-Daro continues to guard many of its secrets. As one of the most advanced urban centers of the Bronze Age, it has yielded immense knowledge, yet equally provoked profound mysteries. Scholars, archaeologists, linguists, and historians still grapple with unanswered questions that resist easy resolution.

This final chapter addresses the significant gaps in our understanding, outlines promising directions for future research, and reflects on how interdisciplinary approaches and emerging technologies could help illuminate this ancient civilization. As we look ahead, we are reminded that Mohenjo-Daro is not only a window into the past, but also a horizon for future discovery.

1. The Indus Script: A Language Still Silent

The most enduring enigma of Mohenjo-Daro—and the Indus Valley Civilization at large—is its undeciphered script. Comprising hundreds of signs, the script appears on seals, pottery, amulets, and tablets, often in short sequences.

Unanswered Questions:

- Is the script a full-fledged language or a system of proto-writing?

- What language or language family does it represent?

- Why are there no long inscriptions, as in Mesopotamian or Egyptian systems?

The Indus script remains uncracked despite attempts using AI, linguistic modeling, and comparative analysis. Future breakthroughs may depend on discovering a bilingual inscription (like the Rosetta Stone) or new computational techniques.

2. Political and Social Organization: A Civilization Without Kings?

Unlike contemporary civilizations, Mohenjo-Daro reveals no monumental palaces, temples, or tombs of kings. This absence raises crucial questions about its governance and social order.

Areas of Inquiry:

- Was there a centralized state or a decentralized network of city-states?

- What roles did priests, merchants, or councils play in decision-making?

- How was law, order, and economic exchange regulated without visible authority symbols?

The mystery deepens when considering how such a vast urban civilization functioned efficiently with minimal signs of violence, conquest, or hierarchy, at least archaeologically.

3. Religion and Belief Systems: Symbols Without Scripture

Mohenjo-Daro lacks decipherable religious texts or clear mythological narratives despite a rich material culture.

Open Questions:

- What were the dominant spiritual beliefs of the people?
- Was there a priesthood, organized religion, or more localized cults and rituals?
- How should we interpret the "Great Bath," phallic symbols,

mother goddess figurines, and animal motifs?

Some scholars suggest early forms of Hindu beliefs, while others warn against projecting later traditions backward. More research is needed to distinguish between ritual symbolism and utilitarian function.

4. Causes of Decline: A Puzzle of Many Pieces

While numerous theories exist—from climate change to river shifts, invasions, or internal collapse—the precise cause of Mohenjo-Daro's decline remains unresolved.

Future research directions:

- Geoarchaeology to study changing river courses (e.g., the drying of the Ghaggar-Hakra system).

- Paleoclimatology is used to reconstruct climate patterns and drought cycles.
- Bioarchaeology and DNA studies to assess migration, health, and population continuity.

Understanding why a thriving, well-planned city was abandoned could offer vital lessons for modern urban resilience and sustainability.

5. Daily Life and Culture: More Than Buildings and Seals

While Mohenjo-Daro's architecture and artifacts reveal much, daily life—especially of **ordinary people **- remains largely invisible.

Questions worth exploring:

- What did people eat, wear, celebrate, and believe in daily?
- How were gender roles, family structures, and childhood experienced?
- What kinds of stories, music, or oral traditions might have shaped their world?

New methods such as residue analysis, micro archaeology, and ethnoarchaeological comparisons may bring these invisible aspects to light.

6. Connections with Other Civilizations: An Incomplete Web

Mohenjo-Daro's artifacts suggest trade with Mesopotamia, Central Asia, and possibly even the Persian Gulf, but the full extent of its global connections is unknown.

Key research goals:

- Map trade routes through maritime archaeology and satellite imaging.

- Study the distribution of Indus-style artifacts abroad to trace influence and interaction.

- Explore cultural exchange in terms of technology, ideas, and social practices.

Were the Indus people passive traders, or did they play an active role in shaping ancient globalization?

7. Technological Capabilities: Ahead of Their Time?

Mohenjo-Daro's urban grid, drainage systems, fired bricks, and water management are marvels of early engineering.

Future research can ask:

- How were these technologies developed and transmitted across cities?
- What tools, measurements, or building protocols were used?
- Can we replicate their methods to learn more about Bronze Age construction science?

Modern-day engineers continue to study the site for insights into sustainable design, flood control, and low-energy architecture.

8. The People of Mohenjo-Daro: Who Were They?

Finally, the question of identity—who built and lived in Mohenjo-Daro—remains partially answered.

Investigations ahead:

- Ancient DNA (aDNA) and isotope analysis to study ancestry, health, and migration patterns.
- Cranial morphology and skeletal studies to identify demographic trends and diseases.
- Population modeling estimates how many people live in the city and how they organize themselves spatially.

Were the Indus people related to modern South Asian populations? Did they migrate elsewhere or assimilate? The answers remain tantalizingly out of reach.

Conclusion: The City That Still Speaks

Mohenjo-Daro may appear still and silent, but it continues to speak through the questions it raises, urging us to look deeper, think broader, and connect across disciplines. It is a reminder that archaeology is not just about the past—it is a dialogue with the present and a quest for understanding that never truly ends.

As we progress, new technologies, discoveries, and theories will reshape our understanding. However, perhaps the most significant revelation Mohenjo-Daro offers is not in what we know but in what we have yet to uncover.

The mystery of Mohenjo-Daro endures, and with it, the promise that humanity's most incredible stories are still unfolding beneath the surface.

CONCLUSION: LEGACY OF THE INDUS VALLEY CIVILIZATION

As we draw the journey of Mohenjo-Daro and the broader Indus Valley Civilization to a close, we are left not with finality, but with a deeper appreciation for the richness, complexity, and enigma of this ancient world. From its meticulously planned cities to its sophisticated crafts, from the enduring silence of its script to the mystery of its disappearance, the Indus civilization stands as one of humanity's great foundational cultures—a silent yet profound pillar of early urban life.

1. A Civilization Ahead of Its Time

Four thousand years ago, while many parts of the world still dwelt in rudimentary village life, the cities of the Indus Valley were already engaging in:

- Advanced urban planning with grid-like street layouts, multi-storied homes, and elaborate drainage systems.

- Sophisticated engineering is seen in the Great Bath, granaries, wells, and water storage infrastructure.

- Long-distance trade networks connected them with Mesopotamia, Central Asia, and possibly the Persian Gulf.

- Standardized systems for weights, measures, brick dimensions, and even urban proportions, suggesting a culture of precision, order, and cooperation.

Unlike other ancient civilizations, the Indus people left no grand monuments to war or kings, but instead, they invested in civic life, shared infrastructure, and balanced design. Their achievements reflect technical expertise and a philosophy of community-centered living—a quiet brilliance still resonates today.

2. Lessons in Sustainability and Equality

Modern scholars often marvel at how the Indus cities functioned with minimal signs of social inequality, warfare, or authoritarian rule. While we cannot claim a utopia, the archaeological evidence points toward:

- Decentralized governance, possibly through merchant guilds, civic councils, or shared rule.

- Balanced social organization, with neighborhoods organized around communal wells, workshops, and equal-sized housing blocks.

- Eco-sensitive construction, using locally available materials, passive cooling, and waste management systems that many modern cities struggle to emulate.

These features offer a model for urban sustainability, egalitarianism, and planning that is strikingly relevant to our times, especially in an era of urban overgrowth, climate crises, and social fragmentation.

3. The Value of the Unwritten Story

Perhaps the greatest paradox of the Indus Valley Civilization is that we know so much about how they lived, yet so little about what they believed, felt, or called themselves. Without deciphered texts, their inner world remains largely opaque.

And yet, the silence is not a void—it is a canvas for curiosity, humility, and global collaboration. The fact that such a highly developed civilization existed without monumental inscriptions or royal propaganda speaks volumes. It reminds us that greatness in history is not always accompanied by noise. Sometimes, the quiet civilizations that built peace over power leave the most lasting legacy.

4. Cultural and Global Relevance

The legacy of Mohenjo-Daro and its sister cities is not just regional or academic—it is global. The Indus civilization represents:

- One of the three earliest cradles of civilization, alongside Mesopotamia and Egypt.

- A vital piece of South Asian identity, shared across modern borders and linguistic divides.

- A testament to the human capacity for complex society, long before modern states or empires.

It is a legacy that belongs to all of humanity, offering insights into how we might live more intelligently, harmoniously, and sustainably.

5. An Open Door to the Future

The story of the Indus Valley Civilization is far from complete. Discoveries, technologies, and interdisciplinary approaches will continue to shape and reshape our understanding:

- DNA research, AI-driven decipherment, geo-imaging, and satellite archaeology may reveal more.

- Public awareness, education, and preservation efforts can turn these ancient cities into living classrooms for generations.

- The challenges of climate, cultural loss, and misinterpretation must be met with a renewed global commitment to heritage and science.

In many ways, the civilization that vanished without conquest, without fire, and memory in writing still lingers—as a quiet call to curiosity, respect, and reflection.

Final Thoughts

Mohenjo-Daro and the Indus Valley Civilization represent not just what was, but also what is possible. In their silence, they speak to the resilience of human endeavor. In their ruins, they whisper of unity, balance, and care for the collective. And in their rediscovery, they call upon us to listen more closely to the past, each other, and the planet.

The Indus legacy is not buried beneath soil layers—it lives in the questions we ask, the truths we seek, and the civilizations we continue to build.

www.ingramcontent.com/pod-product-compliance
Lightning Source LLC
Chambersburg PA
CBHW062214080426
42734CB00010B/1890